SPARK YOUR in CAREER

BOOK PUBLISHING

by Traci Maynigo

SPARK NOTES

SPARKNOTES is a registered trademark of SparkNotes LLC

Spark Publishing
A Division of Barnes & Noble
120 Fifth Avenue
New York, NY 10011
www.sparknotes.com

Library of Congress Cataloging-in-Publication Data

Maynigo, Traci, 1981–
  Spark your career in book publishing / written by Traci Maynigo.
    p. cm.
  ISBN-13: 978-1-4114-9812-9
  ISBN-10: 1-4114-9812-7
  1. Publishers and publishing—Vocational guidance—United States. I. Title.

Z471.M39 2007
070.502373—dc22

2006037112

Please submit changes or report errors to www.sparknotes.com/errors.

Printed and bound in the United States.

10 9 8 7 6 5 4 3 2 1

CONTENTS

PART III: CAREER-PLANNING TOOLS

SPARK YOUR CAREER in

BOOK PUBLISHING

FOREWORD

by Jack Romanos

I'd never really thought about publishing, but the minute I
got into it I knew it was the right place to be. I loved books
and I loved reading, and the idea of actually getting *paid* to
be in that environment was intriguing. But even more than
that, I felt like publishing was a business that had an impact
on the culture and was significant to society. I wanted to do
something that mattered.

Books are simply great products. They have an enor-
mous value from both an educational and an entertainment
standpoint: We all know that a good book can change the
world. Plus, they're enduring. If you work in publishing,
you're creating something that can last forever, and that's
incredibly gratifying—far more so than a paycheck could
ever be. After 40 years in the business, I still haven't lost
my drive or my excitement. Every Monday, I can't wait to
see what's on the bestseller lists, and that rush just doesn't
go away.

This is a great time to be getting into publishing, because
the industry is currently poised on the edge of a major shift.

The digital revolution is changing the media landscape. In the 1960s, the emergence of the paperback transformed the publishing business, as baby boomers like me found a format that really connected to our generation. Now, the digital generation is about to revolutionize the industry again, in its own image. e-Books, electronic distribution of content, digital readers, print-on-demand—not to mention new technologies and business models that we can't even conceive of yet—are going to change the entire face of the industry in the years ahead. You can have a hand in shaping that future. If you're a young person who wants a challenging, lifelong career in a thriving, growing industry, book publishing might just be it.

Best of luck to you in your job search!

Jack Romanos
CEO, Simon & Schuster
New York City
2007

INTRODUCTION

Publishing is about more than just hotshot authors and glamorous editors who lunch at Elaine's and call each other "darling." It's about more than Danielle Steele and John Grisham and bestsellers like *The Da Vinci Code* and *Tuesdays with Morrie*. Every year thousands of ideas are turned into manuscripts, deals are negotiated, covers are designed, pages are edited, and author tours are planned. Publishing's full of talented individuals who love, love, *love* books.

Still, breaking into this industry can be tough. If you've picked up this book, we know you've got dreams of making it in publishing. So how are you going to make yourself stand out from the thousands of other starry-eyed hopefuls clutching red pens and copies of their favorite book jackets so that *your* dream is the one that actually becomes a reality? You need to work hard—and read this book.

Spark Your Career in Book Publishing will give you everything you need to make your mark in publishing. You'll get a crash course in how the industry works, including a description of all the major players. You'll also learn how to write a kick-ass résumé and cover letter. This book's got you covered, whether you're looking for tips about scoring a killer internship or about creating a powerful network of professional contacts—even if the only person you know who does anything related to publishing is your cousin who sells used paperbacks at the local flea market.

And we'll be there for you when you land your first job in publishing. We'll show you how to deal with the long hours and grunt work that often characterize those first publishing jobs (sorry—but it's true). Okay, so it isn't always book parties and Pulitzers, but for those who are willing to put in the energy and the effort, a dynamic and exciting career awaits. And we're going to help you get there.

TOP 10 SIGNS YOU WERE BORN TO WORK IN BOOK PUBLISHING

1

Your first-grade teacher had to use a dictionary when reading your homework.

2

When you can't sleep, you count publishers' imprints.

3

You send fan mail to the editors at the *London Review of Books*.

4

You can't wait for the day Fox or NBC announces its latest reality show: *Project Publishing House*.

5

Your idea of a fun Friday night involves Scrabble and the *New York Times* crossword puzzle.

6

You carry a red pencil everywhere to mark typos on street signs, movie posters, and menus.

7

You think Jane Friedman should run for president, with Sonny Mehta as her VP.

8

You plan to name your children Alfred, Scribner, Holtzbrinck, and Simon.

9

When friends come to you for advice, your counsel usually begins with something like, "Your dilemma reminds me of a similar problem Daisy faces in *The Great Gatsby*. . . ."

10

You know what a dangling modifier is.

PART I: INDUSTRY SNAPSHOT

1

HOW IS THE INDUSTRY DIVIDED?

You might anxiously await the next book by Stephen King, or you might prefer to purchase the latest winner of the Pulitzer Prize. Either way, there's more to the book publishing industry than a handful of bestselling or prizewinning authors. A whole lot more, as a matter of fact. More than 150,000 new books are published every year—by established authors, unknown authors, and celebrities, not to mention hundreds of thousands of reprints of older books. The industry promises to keep thriving regardless of technological advancements or economic depressions. Movies, television sitcoms, blog entries, and magazine articles tend to evaporate into the ether rather quickly, but books remain—faithful stalwarts of your shelves, ready for another read. Bottom line: There will always be books, so there will always be jobs in publishing.

In this section, we'll tell you everything you need to know about the publishing industry. First, we'll explain the different types of books that get published each year. Then, we'll cover the different types of publishers who produce those books.

TYPES OF BOOKS

There seems to be no limit to what a book looks like or what it discusses. Cookbooks, encyclopedias, novels, guidebooks, textbooks, photography books—books are printed in a wide range of formats and cover every conceivable topic. You name it, there's a book about it somewhere. Not to mention the countless works of fiction that feed every corner of the imagination, such as suspense, romance, mystery, literary, and fantasy. The possibilities are endless.

But there's no need to be overwhelmed by all these possibilities. Below is a list of the three most common types of books. Everything from dictionaries to graphic novels fits into one of these categories:

- **Trade books**
- **Educational books**
- **Professional books**

Know thyself . . .

What kind of books would you want to work on? First, check out your own bookshelves. Make a list of the titles you hold near and dear. Second, go to a bookstore; grab a coffee or comfy chair and just look through the various books that catch your eye. You might discover that you're really into art books, despite never having taken an art history class, or you might find the complexity of textbooks really interesting. Be open to different possibilities. Finally, check out who publishes the books you own or enjoy by looking at a book's spine or copyright page.

Trade Books

Trade books are the types of books you're probably most familiar with—the ones you buy at a bookstore, purchase online, or check out at the library. They're aimed at the general consumer rather than at a more specialized market, such as scholars or professionals. Sold to libraries, bookstores, and wholesalers or general retailers (such as Costco, Wal-Mart, and Kmart), trade books can be fiction or nonfiction, adult or children's.

FICTION BOOKS

Fiction books are creative, nonfactual works and can generally be divided into two types: literary fiction and popular fiction.

    Literary fiction is considered the highest form of creative writing (it's the kind of writing that usually wins such prizes as the National Book Award and the Pulitzer Prize). Notable for its often intellectual or poetic prose, literary fiction is also valued for its artistic quality and craftsmanship. Most books you read in a high school or in a college literature course,

Those in the know often refer to books as **titles,** as in "our fall titles look spectacular in that new display."

such as works by Ernest Hemingway (*The Sun Also Rises*) or James Joyce (*Ulysses*), fall into this category. Some more recent literary fiction works include *Memoirs of a Geisha,* by Arthur Golden, and *The Namesake,* by Jhumpa Lahiri.

Popular (pop) fiction (also known as commercial fiction) is lighter and often formulaic, written to fit the style of a given **genre,** or category. Some pop fiction authors include John Grisham (*The Broker*), Stephen King (*Cell*), Nora Roberts (*The Circle Trilogy*), and Dan Brown (*The Da Vinci Code*). Recently, however, many writers have combined literary fiction with generic characteristics to form a literary-genre hybrid. This hybrid includes the likes of author Jonathan Lethem (*Motherless Brooklyn*) and editor Michael Chabon (*McSweeney's Treasury of Thrilling Tales*).

The following is a sampling of some pop fiction genres, as listed on BarnesandNoble.com:

- Action and Adventure
- Chick Lit (or Women's Fiction)
- Erotica
- Fairy Tales
- Gay and Lesbian
- Graphic Novels
- Historical Fiction
- Horror
- Mystery and Crime
- Nautical and Maritime Fiction
- Religious and Inspirational
- Romance
- Science Fiction and Fantasy
- Thrillers
- Westerns

Reprints of titles more than a year old are known as **backlist books.** These titles may be fiction or nonfiction, adult or children's. New titles are known as **frontlist books.**

NONFICTION BOOKS

Nonfiction books are works of history, fact, or opinion. They often have complex organizational structures, including sidebars, illustrations, photographs, cross-references, indexes, and appendices. *Spark Your Career in Book Publishing* falls into this category.

How Frey got fried

In 2003, James Frey wrote a memoir of his time in a drug rehab facility, and *A Million Little Pieces* shot up the bestseller charts, particularly after Oprah Winfrey chose it for her book club. As sales climbed into the six figures, some critics at the website TheSmokingGun.com decided to do a little investigating into the truthfulness of Frey's story of drug abuse and redemption. What they found rocked the publishing industry.

In January 2006, Frey admitted that several portions of his book were false. For example, Frey claimed that he spent three months in a maximum-security prison; the Smoking Gun discovered that Frey had spent just a couple of hours in jail. The trouble was that both Frey and his publisher, Random House, had marketed the book as a nonfiction memoir when, in reality, a good portion of the book was fiction. Several bookstores went so far as to reshelve Frey's work in the fiction/literature section as a result of his admissions, and some readers were angry enough to sue Frey and Random House. The case was settled in September 2006, with Frey and his publisher agreeing to refund the money of irate readers who could prove that they'd purchased the book before the maelstrom.

Today, new printings of *A Million Little Pieces* contain a "note to readers" in which Frey admits to fabricating chunks of his story. In fact, just about every memoir published post-Frey contains some type of disclaimer in which the author admits that portions of his or her book might be embellished. Does this mean that every writer who writes an autobiography is an imaginative liar? Nope, not at all. These disclaimers just tell readers the truth: It's difficult to remember verbatim the kinds of conversations or events that make for good reading, particularly when many years have gone by, so sometimes writers have to add a detail, collapse several events into one, or combine characters. Keep that in mind the next time you sit down and read a memoir.

Some bestselling nonfiction books include *How to Buy, Sell, and Profit on eBay*, by Adam Ginsberg; *Confessions of an Economic Hit Man*, by John Perkins; and *The Tipping Point*, by Malcolm Gladwell. Here's a sampling of nonfiction genres, as listed on BarnesandNoble.com:

- Africana
- Art, Architecture, and Photography

- Biography and Memoirs
- Business and Investing
- Computers and Internet
- Cooking, Food, and Wine
- Crafts and Hobbies
- Diet and Health
- Gay and Lesbian
- Health, Mind, and Body
- History
- Home and Garden
- Memoir
- Outdoors and Nature
- Parenting and Families
- Pets
- Politics
- Reference
- Religion
- Science and Nature
- Sports and Adventure
- Study Guides and Test Prep
- Travel
- Women's Studies

CHILDREN'S BOOKS

Children's books appeal to children of all ages, from infants to teenagers, although some adults also read them. Here are some types of children's books.

- **Board books:** Little and often square shaped, these books for infants and toddlers have a small number of thick pages.

- **Picture books:** These books feature pictures or illustrations on every page. The images tell a story using only a few lines of text. Picture books are usually 24 to 32 pages long and target readers between the ages of 2 and 8.

- **Novelty books:** Also known as **movable books,** these have special built-in features like pop-ups, foldout pages, liftable flaps, and hidden sound chips. These books might be any length and generally target readers between the ages of 2 and 8.

- **Concept books:** Using illustrations and a few words per page, these books teach a basic concept, such as letters, numbers, or colors. These books may be any length and generally target readers between the ages of 2 and 8.

- **Early readers:** Also known as **easy readers** and **beginning chapter books,** these books contain a substantial amount of illustrations and controlled vocabulary to help children move on to chapter books. Early readers are usually about 64 pages long and are aimed at readers ages 8 to 11 who are growing out of picture books.

- **Hi/Lo books:** Featuring less challenging text combined with a compelling story (known as "high interest"), these books attempt to coax hesitant readers between the ages of 8 and 15 into more active reading.

- **Chapter books:** These books, for children ages 9 to 12, include one line drawing per chapter, but primarily uses text to tell a story.

- **Middle readers:** With mostly text and few, if any, drawings, these books target readers in grammar and junior high schools (ages 9 to 12). Notable examples of middle readers include *Harry Potter and the Sorcerer's Stone,* by J. K. Rowling, and *Alice's Adventures in Wonderland,* by Lewis Carroll.

- **Juvenile/young adult (YA) books:** These "coming-of-age" novels or nonfiction works focus on such topics as dating, fitting in, friendships, sex, drugs, self-esteem, school, and family relationships. YA books often serve as learning and coping tools for adolescents, usually between the ages of 12 and 18.

BOOK FORMATS

Books not only come in a variety of genres but also in several different formats.

- **Hardcover books** tend to be the most expensive and highest-quality type of book. They're sewn and glued, then bound with cardboard covers, reinforced with a stiff cloth, and covered with a paper dust jacket. Hardcovers may cost anywhere from $24.95 to $40 or more.

- **Trade paperbacks** may either be original books or reprints of books that were originally printed in hardcover. They're bound with glue and a heavy paper cover. Trade paperbacks usually retail for around $15.

- **Mass-market paperbacks** are works of popular fiction that are smaller than trade paperbacks, printed on lower-quality paper, and cheaper to buy (usually $4.99 to $6.99). Sold in high volume through supermarket chains and other retailers, these books tend to be works of romance, true crime, or horror.

- **Audiobooks** are presented in a recorded audio format, either on a compact disc or in the form of an MP3. Many printed books are available in this format and can be purchased online or at a bookstore. Audiobooks are usually more expensive than their printed counterparts but are popular among consumers who might not have time to read.

- **e-Books** are stored in a virtual library, then distributed and read in an electronic format. They're usually purchased and downloaded online as a digital file and read on a computer or on a personal digital assistant (PDA) screen. e-Books are especially helpful for college students, who can easily store and access thousands of pages of reference materials rather than having to lug around textbooks. This format is also slowly starting to replace the print format in the arena of professional and scholarly publishing.

Educational Books

Educational books include textbooks, teaching manuals and aids, workbooks, guides, computer and online programs, and audiovisuals. Basically, anything that helps teachers teach and students learn falls into this category of book publishing. There are three types of educational books.

- **Elementary and high school (el-hi) textbooks** are purchased by school systems and given to the students for free to use during the academic year.

- **College or higher-education textbooks** are adopted by professors or academic departments, and then purchased directly by the students at college, local, or online bookstores.

- **Study aids** are used by students to bone up for a particular course or to prepare for a standardized test such as the SAT or the GRE.

e-Educational publishing

Many educators think e-books would be the cheapest, most efficient format for textbooks in elementary and high schools. However, since the United States is not 100 percent computerized (hard to believe, isn't it?), some people argue that converting to e-books would create electronic "haves and have-nots," a situation that would be unethical and unfair.

The case may be different, though, for college educational publishing. College textbooks continue to be extremely costly, so many students buy used textbooks or share books with their classmates. As more and more colleges require that every student purchase a computer, textbook publishers will probably soon sell their textbooks online rather than in print.

Professional Books

Designed for working professionals, **professional books** serve as educational tools in specific careers and trades. They're sold to large professional organizations, such as hospitals, law firms, research institutions, and accounting practices. Published by members of the International Association of Scientific, Technical & Medical Publishers (known as **STM publishers**) and the Association of Learned and Professional Society Publishers (ALPSP), professional books include legal citations, regulatory compliance materials, practical publications, directories, and professional journals. And they cover a wide range of specific topics, including (but not limited to) medicine, mathematics, statistics, physics, optics, engineering, law, business, computers, and accounting. Examples of STM books include *Pathology of the Human Placenta,* by Kurt Benirschke et al., and *Copyright and the Public Interest,* by Gillian Davies.

❝❝ What I like about the book publishing industry is that, from my experience, the players involved are all very human. We work very reasonable hours, and a lot of concessions are made for employees when life gets in the way of work.

"What I dislike about the industry in general is that it's quite incestuous. The same people tend to move from one company to the next and then back again. A common warning is that the rear end you kick one day may be the rear end you kiss the next."

—**Rebecca J. Ortman,** Market Research Analyst
Pearson Longman English Language Training

TYPES OF PUBLISHERS

Now you know all about the different types of books that come out each year. Next we'll explain all you need to know about book publishers. With so many different types of books, it's not surprising that, according to the *Literary Market Place,* a gigantic tome that lists names and addresses of publishers and agents, there are currently 53,000 book publishers in the United States, with staff sizes ranging from one to tens of thousands.

Spending your days working on books that you'd like to read at home isn't a bad way to make a living, so this section explains who publishes what. But with so many publishers, we couldn't mention each and every one. *Writer's Market,* published annually, lists just about every publisher in the United States, along with information about what they publish and whom to contact about placing a piece or selling a proposal. Check it out. And read on to see how to turn your love of books into a job you'll love.

The chart below lists the five major types of publishers, along with the types of books they publish (in order of primacy) and some examples of recent bestsellers. As you'll see, there's lots of overlap between the type of publisher and the type of book published.

Type of Publisher	Type of Book Published	Example
Commercial publishing houses	Trade, professional, educational	*The Devil Wears Prada* (novel published by Anchor)
Small presses	Trade, professional, educational	*Fullmetal Alchemist* (manga published by Viz Media)
University presses	Educational, professional, trade	*Historical Statistics of the United States* (multivolume hard-covers published by Cambridge University Press)
Professional and scholarly publishers	Professional, educational, trade	*Videoblogging* (nonfiction paperback published by John Wiley & Sons)
Educational publishers	Educational, professional, trade	*Prego!* (Italian textbook published by McGraw-Hill)

Publishing companies are usually referred to as **houses,** as in "SparkNotes' house style requires writers to use the serial comma and to send their editors lots of chocolate."

Location, Location, Location

Few publishing professionals will deny it: When it comes to book publishing, New York City is the heart of it all. Most of the major commercial, professional and scholarly, and educational publishers are headquartered in New York City or at least have corporate or satellite offices in Manhattan. Even some university presses, such as Oxford, have branches in the city.

But don't fret if you'd rather live elsewhere. Opportunities for careers in publishing aren't only limited to New York City. Every state has publishers, including university presses and small presses, which offer similar opportunities in less competitive environments. You may not be working on the next bestseller at these houses, but you'll likely have a more diverse experience—and you might even move up faster. Here is a (very incomplete) list of some successful publishers based outside of New York City:

- Algonquin Books, Chapel Hill, NC
- Apogee Press, Berkeley, CA
- Beacon Press, Boston, MA
- Candlewick Press, Cambridge, MA
- Copper Canyon Press, Port Townsend, WA
- Cornell University Press, Ithaca, NY
- Dalkey Archive Press, Normal, IL
- Graywolf Press, St. Paul, MN
- Posterity Press, Chevy Chase, MD
- Princeton University Press, Princeton, NJ
- Republic Books, Fredericksburg, TX
- Sourcebooks, Chicago, IL
- University Press of Kansas, Lawrence, KS
- Willow Creek Press, Minocqua, WI

COMMERCIAL PUBLISHING HOUSES

Commercial publishing houses probably published many of the books that live on your bookshelves or that tend to catch your eye at bookstores. Frequently owned by a gigantic media conglomerate, commercial publishing houses tend to be the largest and most corporately structured of all publishing companies. Commercial publishers choose what to publish based on consumer trends, and they generally handle all aspects of the publishing process in-house, from editing to designing to printing to distributing to promoting and marketing.

Expect to come across all possible types of books at a big publishing house. Every season, big houses publish a cluster of **celebrity books,** or books by or about well-known personalities or well-established authors. The guaranteed success of these (sometimes less literary but always very popular) titles give big publishing houses the wiggle room to take risks on books by no-name authors or on esoteric subjects. Celebrity books and a strong backlist give commercial houses the money to float the less popular books or less successful imprints.

> ### Brand-name imprints
>
> Commercial publishing houses are so large that they're divided into **imprints,** or specific lines of books. Each imprint has its own personality, and its books usually focus on a select few genres, subjects, or formats. The imprint name functions like a brand, often indicating a certain level of quality associated with the titles and authors it publishes. Knopf, for example, is an imprint of Random House and publishes distinguished and classic fiction and nonfiction. Another Random House imprint, Fodor's, publishes travel guides.

Personality Profile

At large commercial houses, you'll find a rigid hierarchy in which every level pays attention to the bottom line. If you fit the following profile, you'll fit right in.

- **You love to read . . . anything and everything.** The imprint you work for may only publish a certain kind of book—inspirational books, for example, or science fiction. If you can see the value in every book—from romance novel to suspense novel, from cookbook to picture book—you'll love life at a big commercial house.

- **You value defined roles and hierarchies.** Commercial houses are highly structured, which means everyone has a specific set of responsibilities. Whatever particular area of publishing you start off in—be it editorial, production and manufacturing, design, marketing and publicity, or sales—expect to jump headfirst into that role and become very skilled at it. Once you demonstrate your abilities, you can start climbing the corporate ladder.

- **You can work fast and under pressure—without sacrificing quality.** Consumers are demanding, so big publishers need to be too. The time between manuscript and printed book is often very brief (sometimes as short as three or four months). Big houses put books on tight schedules to ensure that publications coincide with current events and fast-changing consumer trends. Deadlines are tight and strict, but quality is just as important as timeliness.

- **You're just not that into . . . money.** While the big publishers promise more financial success for you than smaller presses in the long run, they also pretty much guarantee a slow climb from the bottom up. Let's face it, though, you aren't in the publishing industry to get rich. You're in it because you love books, not money!

66 Go to work in publishing because you love to read and want to work on reading materials for others, not because you plan to get rich. Some writers/editors do all right financially, but you can probably find quicker ways to make a million."

—**Karen Taschek,** Editor/Writer
Taschek Trade and Tech

Job Culture

Here's what you can expect at a big commercial house when you're just starting out.

- **There's paper everywhere.** Big houses run like machines, and every piece matters. Each task you carry out at the bottom— including menial stuff such as photocopying, mailing materials, and filling out forms—is just as indispensable as any decision the CEO makes. You'll have to do your part to help produce a quality book that satisfies everyone involved, from editors to customers. Doing so, though, usually involves reams and reams of paper, including manuscripts and page proofs, all of which must be printed, organized, and filed.

- **You'll work extra hours—and have homework.** You may start out your publishing career spending much of your time lugging around manuscripts, but you also get to read them. Because the manuscripts pile up, you might have to take some home with you to read on your own time. But who doesn't love a good book on the subway or at home before going to bed, especially if you get to read it before everyone else does?

- **You'll get free books and then some!** Let's be honest: You want into this industry for the free books, right? Commercial houses offer other great perks: competitive benefits, discounts on movies and Broadway shows, a fair amount of vacation days, and, often, half-day Fridays in the summertime. You may even get to meet a bestselling author or two.

- **You'll work hard, then play hard.** Publishing houses are busy places, but they're also extremely social. You'll soon have a new group of friends who all share that same love of books and reading that you do. And you can hit the happy hours together to talk shop and stock up on free food.

The Major Players

The first step to landing a job at any publishing house is to brush up on the company and its competitors. Learn who owns it, who runs it, and, most important, what books it publishes and which ones are bestsellers. Below are a few tidbits about some of the major players.

- **Random House,** randomhouse.com
  The largest English-language general trade book publisher in the world, Random House is a division of Bertelsmann AG, the German media conglomerate that also owns BMG, the umbrella corporation of Sony BMG Music Entertainment and BMG Music Publishing. Some of Random House's bestsellers include *Beloved*, by Toni Morrison; *H. R. H.*, by Danielle Steele; and *The Year of Magical Thinking*, by Joan Didion.

- **Penguin Group,** us.penguingroup.com
  The second-largest English-language trade book publisher in the world, the Penguin Group is a division of Pearson, the English media group that also owns the *Financial Times* and Pearson Education. Recent

bestsellers include *Collapse,* by Jared Diamond; *The Wal-Mart Effect,* by Charles Fishman; and *The Kite Runner,* by Khaled Hosseini.

- **HarperCollins Publishers,** harpercollins.com
HarperCollins is the third-largest English-language trade publisher in the world and a subsidiary of Australian conglomerate News Corporation, which also owns the film studio 20th Century Fox, the *New York Post,* and all Fox TV stations. Its recent bestsellers include *Freakonomics,* by Steven D. Levitt and Stephen J. Dubner; *Wicked,* by Gregory Maguire; and *Secrets of the Millionaire,* by T. Harv Eker.

- **Simon & Schuster,** simonsays.com
A division of the U.S. international media company Viacom Inc. (owner of Comedy Central, MTV, BET, Nickelodeon, Paramount Pictures, and hundreds of others), Simon & Schuster publishes a variety of general interest books worldwide. Some Simon & Schuster bestsellers include *Daddy's Little Girl,* by Mary Higgins Clark; *The Sum of All Fears,* by Tom Clancy; and *The 7 Habits of Highly Effective People,* by Steven R. Covey.

Independent publishers

Independent publishers differ from commercial publishing houses in that they tend to be privately owned rather than owned by a media conglomerate or stockholders. Without a corporation harping on the bottom line, independent publishers often have the flexibility to take risks and not be so financially driven. They can be as large as commercial publishing houses and are often just as successful. Lonely Planet, for example, has become the world's leading travel publisher, with more than 600 titles in print in English that describe traveling to countless destinations around the world. Workman Publishing, another major leading independent publisher, is recognized for its innovative formats and packaging, as well as its growing collection of calendars in various shapes and styles. This publisher's books and other products are characteristically both enduring (*What to Expect When You're Expecting,* by Arlene Eisenberg and Heidi E. Murkoff) and idiosyncratic (*The Official Preppy Handbook,* by Lisa Birnbach).

SMALL PRESSES

If you imagine the publishing world as a giant wrestling match, the big commercial houses are the defending champions, while the small presses are the tough and sly underdogs. It's a good thing for all concerned, though, that publishing is really nothing like wrestling; after all, could you imagine editing books while wearing those tights?

Small presses usually have between 3 and 40 employees and publish between 8 and 70 titles a year. Usually privately owned, they tend to publish books devoted to one or two particular subjects or, sometimes, just one or two books per year. Rather than relying on guaranteed commercial bestsellers in fiction and nonfiction, small presses stay afloat by developing books to fit the needs of **niche,** or tightly focused, markets. One small press, for example, might publish only SAT test preparation guidebooks, while another might only do books about woodworking (no, seriously). These books probably won't hit the bestseller lists, but they will always have a solid market: Every year a new batch of high school students will need help studying for the SAT, and some people are more devoted to their hobbies than to their spouses. Because they offer smaller advances to their authors, small presses don't generally attract the big names. To cut costs, they print fewer books at a time. Small presses also use non-traditional sales outlets that fit their niche markets, such as home improvement stores, gardening stores, sporting goods stores, and children's stores. For example, Soft Skull Press might try to sell a book about punk rock politics at the merchandising table at a rock concert.

Personality Profile

Does size matter? Read on to figure out whether you're a good fit for a small house.

- **Awesome, high-quality books mean more to you than $$$.** Small presses don't necessarily strive to publish the next bestseller. They simply want to nurture their authors and help them publish high-quality books that might otherwise be overlooked by major publishers.

Small presses handle every book and author with care, and the author is the utmost priority. If you want to help produce books for the sake of their artistic value or service to a particular consumer need rather than for their salability, definitely consider working for a small press.

- **You long to know everything about publishing.** With fewer books to publish, fewer employees, and no parent company to answer to, small presses have less need for a rigid hierarchical structure than do commercial publishing houses. Instead of being a cog in a machine, you'll more likely have the opportunity to dabble in every stage of the process. Doing so means you'll gain a better understanding of how the big publishing "machine" works. If you strive to become a publishing jack-of-all-trades, a small press is a great place to start.

- **You love solving problems creatively and enjoy juggling a wide range of projects.** The diversity of books at some small presses guarantees a diversity of challenges as well. You'll be working on books of all shapes and sizes, which means you'll have to perform many functions on a daily basis. Working on an organic cookbook, for example, will present challenges different from working on a photography book. Problems will always come up that you've never encountered before, and you'll have to solve them gracefully.

- **You're innovative, perseverant, and entrepreneurial.** Without the financial backing of a parent company or the guarantee of a bestseller, small presses imaginatively try to cut costs and sell their books. But their employees truly care about each book they publish, and this passion motivates them to persevere. If you're endlessly inventive and never give up, you'll fit in at a small press.

Job Culture

So what's it really like? Read on, friends.

- **You'll participate in the care and feeding of authors.** Small presses really care about their authors, so you're more likely to cross paths with them here than at a big commercial house. Putting the author first can be a blessing and a curse. Author interaction is a big plus: You'll be exposed to unique creative energy and develop relationships that can be very inspiring and stimulating. However, many authors take their art very seriously and can be demanding. Giving them more attention can mean a lot of extra work for you.

- **You'll have passionate and energetic coworkers.** Those who work at independent presses are driven by their passion for the books they work on. They invest deeply in their projects, and the work environment reflects this energy. The publishing team may be much smaller at these presses, but you'll soon develop a close-knit group of friends, with the common bond of working on books you all feel proud of.

- **You'll get variety, variety, variety.** You won't find the inflexible structure of a commercial house here. Fewer books and less money mean fewer employees taking on more responsibilities. Rather than becoming a specialist in a particular skill, you'll likely become knowledgeable about many aspects of the publishing process. Plus, you'll be working on such a wide range of books that you'll never get bored.

- **You'll have more room for creativity.** Without the pressure from a media conglomerate to find the next bestseller, small presses can get a little more creative. This means you can get creative too. Without structure, and with such a wide range of projects and very little money to work with, you'll have to develop all sorts of strategies to publicize your books.

The Major Players

As with the commercial publishers, you need to do some research on small presses before you go in for an interview. Find out who does what, who competes with whom, who writes for whom, and what everyone's bestsellers are. Because these publishers often cater to very specific markets, you also need to know something about the target audience. Remember that *small* doesn't mean *invisible*. Some small presses get noticed in the publishing scene and frequently come out with titles that get people talking. Here's a list of a few major players and their breakout books.

- **Health Communications Inc.,** hci-online.com
Regarded as "the life issues" publisher, this Florida-based small press first got noticed in 1983 with the *New York Times*–bestselling *Adult Children of Alcoholics,* by Dr. Janet Woititz. Continuing in the self-help and inspirational vein, HCI made an even bigger mark in 1994 with *Chicken Soup for the Soul,* which not only hit the bestseller list but also became an international phenomenon. Now HCI publishes more than 500 titles on inspiration, self-help, soul/spirituality, relationships, recovery/healing, and women's issues.

- **Chelsea Green Publishing,** chelseagreen.com
Based in White River Junction, Vermont, this small publisher prides itself on publishing books that promote sustainable living. Chelsea Green's bestsellers include *Don't Think of an Elephant,* by George Lakoff, and *The Straw Bale House,* by Bill Steen et al. Founded in 1984, Chelsea Green now has more than 200 titles in print, some selling roughly 250,000 copies each.

- **Quirk Books,** quirkbooks.com
This Philadelphia small press publishes "impractical reference and irreverent nonfiction" that aims "to amuse, to bemuse, to entertain, and to inform." David Borgenicht founded Quirk Books, as well as coauthored of one of their most successful titles, *Worst-Case Scenario Survival Handbook*. This little paperback has generated several sequels, calendars, T-shirts, a television series, and even a board game.

- **Alice James Press,** www.alicejamesbooks.org
Founded in 1973, this small publisher, based in Farmington, Maine, runs as a **collective** (meaning that a group of people make all the decisions relating to the house). It only publishes poetry, but its authors have won such major awards as the Lenore Marshall Poetry Prize. Not-able poets published by Alice James include Cole Swenson and Jane Kenyon.

- **Drawn and Quarterly,** drawnandquarterly.com
This small Canadian house is devoted to all things comic and graphic. Since its founding in 1992, D+Q has published more than 100 comic

books, art books, sketchbooks, and graphic novels, in addition to a well-regarded annual magazine anthology of new work by artists and designers. It averages around 20 titles per year.

You're a kid at heart and want to work with like-minded souls

Find a home at a children's book publisher! Thanks to the success of the Harry Potter franchise, the children's market continues to grow, and children's books are hot, hot, hot. Publishing professionals often advise novices to choose which type of publishing they want to work in, whether children's or adult, early on. Several characteristics set children's book publishing apart from adult book publishing.

- Children's books are heavily visual, so their editors need to have a strong sense of design as well as content.

- They're largely marketed to public and school libraries in addition to bookstores.

- Last but not least, children's books require a keen sense of what a young audience will respond to. As illustrator Maurice Sendak put it, "Those who write, illustrate, and publish children's books have to work from the thoughts and feelings of the children they once were, who are still alive within them."

Many publishing houses have created children's imprints, and other publishers, such as Scholastic, publish only children's books. Wherever you end up, you'll no doubt be working with people teeming with youthful energy. Many will already have experience teaching or working with children in some respect, and some may seem like big kids themselves. Plus, creating all sorts of tools and products meant for children means you might feel like your work environment resembles a grown-up playground.

UNIVERSITY PRESSES

University presses publish academic titles for universities, colleges, high schools, junior high schools, and independent scholars. With a strong commitment to scholarship, these houses began as vehicles for publishing tracts and dissertations written for and by the faculties of their associated schools. Gradually, presses at various universities extended their efforts beyond their campuses, with the goal of producing serious nonfiction works that serve the needs of professors and academic experts, as well as interested mainstream readers.

University presses resemble small presses in that they print smaller quantities and give smaller advances to their authors. Like commercial houses tied to major media conglomerates, though, university presses are an extension of a parent institution, namely the university with which they're associated. University presses are subsidized by their parent institutions and are generally not-for-profit (this means that they're under no pressure to, and in fact are prohibited from, making a profit under IRS guidelines). Nevertheless, university presses watch the bottom line, and they don't publish books that won't sell.

For the most part, university presses publish scholarly works of nonfiction in a wide array of disciplines, including economics, philosophy, literary criticism, and history. However, many have begun to publish trade books that reflect a certain level of scholarship but still appeal to mainstream readers, such as books of poetry, narrative history, and translations of fiction first published in Europe or Asia. Some presses have even ventured into the commercial trade market, with a few of their books hitting the *New York Times* bestseller list, including Harvard University Press's *The Black Book of Communism,* by Stéphane Courtoi et al., and Oxford University Press's *The Sea Around Us,* by Rachel Carson.

Personality Profile

Should you put the "you" in *university*? Definitely, if these statements describe you.

- **You're hot for teacher—and school.** If you consider college to be the best four years of your life (and not because you partied too hard to pass your classes but because you actually *liked* studying), consider working for a university press. Here, you'll serve the very academic environment you enjoyed during college. You'll love it at a university press if you're thrilled by the idea of working on books written by prominent professors or on books of significant scholastic quality.

- **You think noncorporate niches are nice.** University presses are unique in that they publish books only meant to serve a niche market (like a small press), but they don't generally seek to make a huge profit from their products (as commercial houses do). That said, university presses do have marketing and sales teams that attend conferences, prepare mailings, and just generally try to get their company's books into the hands of eager buyers. No company can keep running without making money—it's just that university presses are less corporate than big commercial houses.

- **You have shrines to scholars in your house.** Professors and scholars are the VIPs at university presses. University presses publish works by and for academics, so you'll be constantly mixing and mingling with well-educated, innovative thinkers and intellectuals. Also, many of your coworkers will have advanced degrees, such as master's or doctorates, so expect some intense conversations around the coffee machine.

66 It helps to have liked school, since you're working with and for academics. But even if you weren't the biggest brain, you can still enjoy working for a university press. I didn't love college, and I like working at a university press."

—**Kyle Capogna,** Marketing/Sales Assistant
Cambridge University Press

Job Culture

- **It's like school but better.** If chatting it up with super-smarties sounds like your bag, you'll fit in quite nicely. Because university presses have strong affiliations with their parent institutions, expect to be integrated into the academic community. You'll probably hang out with many professors and scholars who might be intimidating if you're not used to this sort of scene. But even intellectuals like to cut loose and talk about the latest reality shows once in a while. Chats here won't be all Sartre, all the time.

- **You'll deal in dollars and sense.** With little more than basic subsidizing from their parent institution, university presses often have to find ways to cut costs. Ivy League schools and other prominent presses tend to offer the most money and job security, even though they likely won't be able to pay their employees as much as some of the large commercial publishing houses. If you're looking for big bucks, frankly, you won't enjoy the smaller paychecks usually found at university presses.

- **You'll be making books perfect—and saleable.** A commitment to scholarship naturally fosters a workplace that strives for nothing less than perfection in terms of the content and quality of their books. Much time and money is spent on creating the ideal scholarly product. But no publisher, including university presses, will put out a book without first considering whether that book will sell. The fact is that all publishers care about profits. Even the most highfalutin scholarly tome has to be marketable to get published.

The Major Players

Here's a list of some big UPs, but there are literally hundreds more.

- **Oxford University Press,** www.oup.com/us
  The world's largest university press, Oxford University Press was founded in the United Kingdom in 1478, making it the oldest publishing house in the English-speaking world. The New York City branch, which opened in 1895, began as a publisher primarily of biblical works and remained as such until the 1930s. Now Oxford publishes scholarly works in such subject areas as business, humanities, social sciences, medicine, and music. The New York office has to report to "delegates," or scholars appointed by Oxford University, which also selects the press's principal officers and owns all of its stock. Some successful books include *The Oxford Companion to American Literature*, edited by James D. Hart, and *The Oxford Book of American Verse*, edited by Richard Ellmann. Oxford also has ventured into trade hardcover and paperback (with its Galaxy Books imprint) and won success with *The Strange Career of Jim Crow*, by C. Vann Woodward, among other titles.

- **Cambridge University Press,** cambridge.org/us

  Another oldie but goodie, Cambridge University Press publishes more than 2,000 titles by approximately 24,000 authors each year. CUP published John Milton and Isaac Newton back in the day; today it publishes educational and trade books in such subjects as computer science, history, and psychology. CUP was founded by a charter granted by England's Henry VIII in 1534, and the New York office has been around since 1949. One of the many notable series and books published by this press is the Cambridge Companion series, which collects foundational essays by important scholars on one huge subject, such as modernism or critical theory.

- **University of Chicago Press,** press.uchicago.edu

  Owned and operated by the university, the University of Chicago Press is most widely known for *The Chicago Manual of Style*. Now in its fifteenth edition, this tome is the bible of the publishing industry. In addition to publishing scholarly nonfiction on a variety of subjects (education, literature, economics, the sciences, sociology, anthropology, political science, business, economics, history, philosophy, linguistics, classics, and literature), this university press has also embarked into the trade market, with successes such as Richmond Lattimore's translation of the *Iliad*, Milton Friedman's *Capitalism and Freedom*, and Kate Turabian's *A Manual for Writers of Term Papers, Theses, and Dissertations*.

- **Harvard University Press,** www.hup.harvard.edu

  After a few centuries of serving just the internal needs of the college, printing books and pamphlets for faculty and students, Harvard University Press relaunched itself in 1913 with three goals: to enhance Harvard's academic reputation, to substantively contribute to the advancement of scholarship at Harvard and throughout the United States, and to make available noncommercial books that would otherwise go ignored without Harvard's backing. And boy, has this press met those goals. HUP continues to publish works of general interest in medicine, natural sciences, humanities, and social and behavioral sciences, while also producing books of contemporary poetry and fiction, memoirs, **festschriften** (collections of writings by several authors as a tribute to a scholar), and symposia. A few successes include *The Double Helix,* by James D. Watson; *The Great Chain of Being,* by Arthur Lovejoy; and important works by Jean Piaget, Emily Dickinson, and Ezra Pound.

PROFESSIONAL AND SCHOLARLY PUBLISHERS

Have you ever wondered who makes sure doctors, lawyers, engineers, and other professionals are kept up-to-date on the latest research in their fields? Professional and scholarly publishers produce books and journals specifically written for and marketed to professionals in a wide variety of industries, including medicine, law, business, technology, science, and the humanities. Often referred to as STM publishing, these publishers produce information in a variety of formats and packages. Disciplines are usually subdivided: Engineering, for example, is divided into electrical, chemical, civil, and mechanical.

Professional publishers must be current in order to satisfy the demands of their readers, who rely on these publications to stay in the know. As such, professional publishers follow the research in various specialized fields. Editors regularly attend annual conferences and meetings held by each STM organization. There, they meet with new and current authors or specialists to develop book ideas based on speeches, lectures, or research.

Once the idea has been hammered out and the book written, professional and scholarly publishers print in low quantities. They do this for two reasons: Markets are limited for such specialized works, and the works get outdated quickly, often within a year or two. To stay up-to-date, publishers frequently rely on electronic and online formats, which are easy to change. They also often release books with spiral bindings, which can be updated by inserting updated pages rather than reprinting an entire volume. Finally, STM publishers usually produce paperbacks rather than hardcovers because hardcovers are more expensive to print and paperback reprints can happen quickly and cheaply.

Professional and scholarly publishers often produce **monographs,** or short books of concentrated statements or summations of research findings.

Personality Profile

Scientifically speaking, here's how to determine whether you'd be happy working at a professional or scholarly house.

- **You're into all things technical, medical, or scientific.** In fact, if you weren't planning on pursuing a career in publishing, you may have studied to become a scientist, doctor, engineer, or some other highly technical profession. Well, lucky for you, at a scholarly publishing house, you can have the best of both worlds. You'll be working on the very books that these professionals learn from to enrich their careers.

- **You dig jargon.** Professional and scholarly books are highly specialized, which means you may not be familiar with many of the subject areas they cover. Every field comes with its own language. If you dislike vocabulary or if you worry about getting frustrated with having to learn, basically, a whole new way of speaking and writing, you may not feel comfortable working for a professional publisher.

- **You've got an eye for detail.** You will be working on complicated books, including some very lengthy reference books with complicated indexes, appendices, charts, and illustrations. These projects require a great deal of organization and attention to detail.

Job Culture

- **You'll be dealing with matters of minutiae.** Professional and scholarly books are probably the most complex and specialized of all types of books. You'll spend your days (and many nights) working out very tiny but very important details. If you don't have a natural inclination for the subject areas the house publishes (and even if you do), you may feel mentally exhausted at the end of the day. On the flip side, you'll be an integral part of helping professionals stay informed and, well, professional.

- **You'll be especially specialized.** Expect to learn a lot about specific subject areas. Heck, you'll probably become as knowledgeable and specialized as the professionals themselves! But in return for this specialization comes little variety: You'll be working on the same subject again and again.

- **You'll have tight deadlines and few long-lasting books.** Since the main concern for professional publishers is to print the most up-to-date research and information, deadlines are tight in order for the books to be current. And most professional books have a short shelf life, as the info becomes dated very quickly.

- **You'll privilege information over imagination.** Professional and scholarly publishers care most about giving comprehensive and up-to-date information in specific subjects in a timely fashion and a straightforward format. So information counts more than creativity. These books are less likely to look like works of art, and they're more likely to be simple in design and printed on cheaper paper. That's not to say, however, that the information found in the books doesn't require a great deal of imagination, scholarship, and thoughtfulness, because it totally does.

The Major Players

- **John Wiley & Sons,** wiley.com
  A prominent international professional and scholarly publisher, Wiley publishes print and electronic STM books and journals, as well as professional and consumer books and textbooks. Wiley's resources are also readily available via the Internet in interactive and fully searchable formats. Situated in Hoboken, New Jersey, Wiley also publishes trade books, including the highly popular For Dummies series.

- **Thomson Learning,** thomson.com
  A division of the Canadian international conglomerate Thomson Corporation, Thomson Learning serves both the educational and professional markets, offering adult education and certification materials for corporations, training centers, and individuals.

Headquartered in Stamford, Connecticut, Thomson publishes courseware, test preparation, testing, assessment, and certification materials in areas such as automotive, business, economics, entrepreneurship, finance, health care, marketing, and technology. Thomson is also home to the Arden Shakespeare series.

- **Elsevier,** elsevier.com
  One of the world's leading multimedia publishers of scientific, technical, and health journals, books, electronic products, services, and databases, Elsevier is owned by Reed Elsevier Group, the U.K. conglomerate that also owns Holt, Rinehart and Winston; Steck Vaughan; Harcourt; Mosby; and LexisNexis. Headquartered in New York City, some of Elsevier's highly regarded works include *Gray's Anatomy,* now a professional bible for human anatomy, by Susan Standring, and *The Language of Medicine,* by Davi-Ellen Chabner, a comprehensive reference book for medical terminology.

- **W. W. Norton & Company,** wwnorton.com
  The oldest and largest independent publishing company owned solely by its employees, Norton has been publishing high-quality adult education books as well as college textbooks and professional books, since 1923. Norton's leading titles are on the subjects of psychology, political science, sociology, psychotherapy, and neuroscience. With its main offices in New York City, Norton also publishes trade books, including the acclaimed *The Rise of American Democracy,* by Sean Wilentz, and *In Search of Memory,* by Eric Candel.

EDUCATIONAL PUBLISHERS

Hands down the largest and most profitable houses, educational publishers produce books and materials for classroom use in elementary and secondary schools, as well as colleges. These educational materials include not only textbooks but also tests, solution manuals, study guides, workbooks, teaching aids, software, and online materials. Educational publishers make sure to keep up-to-date on current research in specialized areas so as to publish textbooks that will appeal to teachers and college professors.

Unlike trade books, which are sold through distributors, college-level textbooks are adopted by either a professor or an entire department. In an **individual adoption,** a professor requires students to purchase a particular book for her course, then places a requisition order with the college bookstore. In a **committee adoption,** a department adopts a book as required reading for all students in the department, and the department places the requisition order.

Elementary and secondary school textbooks are adopted through a long and rigid process by state, city, or local school districts or boards of education. Educational publishers, therefore, work closely with school principals and textbook committees consisting of administrators and teachers to make sure their books meet standards demanded by the school systems. The publishers create prototypes based on the school systems' guidelines. Editorial review boards then review the prototypes. Finally, the states adopt the best materials for their school system. There's more money in education publishing, since the profit margin is larger on textbooks. Plus, an adopted textbook usually means a lucrative, long-lasting relationship between the publishers and the school.

Personality Profile

The list below will educate you about whether you're right for a career in educational publishing.

- **If you weren't going into publishing, you'd become a teacher.** Employees at educational publishers may not actually be in the classroom, but they're providing the teaching and learning materials used in the classroom. If you love to help people learn, working at an educational publishing house will probably be a very rewarding experience for you.

- **You understand young learners.** Remember, you'll be molding young people's very impressionable minds. It's important that you're conscientious and sensitive to controversial issues in a subject or discipline. You have to be alert to what language and ideas are appropriate to introduce into a classroom and relevant to the age and interest level of the students. If you know how to shift your creative lens for a young and pliable audience, you'll be a definite asset to an educational publisher.

- **You're into a particular subject area—and you want to develop that passion in others.** Working on textbooks will require significant knowledge in a particular subject. You may be working on textbooks on calculus, American history, world literature, French, physics, or organic chemistry. But in addition to working on a discipline or subject you love, you'll be using your expertise to help educate and inspire students.

- **You've got good design sense.** Working on textbooks requires a sharp eye for detail, as well as a good sense of visual layout. Of course, textbooks need to have the right information, but they also need to attract the reader in a way that stimulates and educates, whether by using timelines, charts, graphs, illustrations—you name it, as long as it helps convey the information.

Job Culture

- **You'll get teamwork, teamwork, teamwork, and more teamwork.** More than any other publishing house, educational publishers require a great amount of teamwork among their employees. Textbooks are very complex and require the work of numerous researchers, writers, scholars, editors, designers, and artists. Not only are the textbooks themselves complex, but they must also be accompanied by myriad teaching and learning materials, including tests, study guides, teaching guides, computer software, and visual and audio tools. Several people help create these materials, and they all must be committed to this cooperative group endeavor.

- **You'll have really strict guidelines and deadlines.** Educational publishers serve a very strict and unique consumer—state, city, or local school districts. These institutions have rigid guidelines for meeting the curricula of their school systems and equally strict deadlines. Their rules for submission are, in most cases, non-negotiable. Textbooks must meet curriculum requirements, as well as fulfill market research needs and demonstrate up-to-date subject matter. Additionally, a textbook often covers a three- to four-year time span (that is, it must be used for three or four years). If a state deadline is missed, the company can't submit the textbook for entry again for another four years.

- **You'll be revising, updating, then updating and revising.** For the most part, once a textbook has established itself in a school system, it will likely remain for several years. So you'll probably spend much of your time revising and updating textbooks that are already staples of school systems. This may mean very little variety for you, but it guarantees that the textbooks are as comprehensive and current as possible.

66 I love books, and I embrace the intellectual nature of working at an educational publisher. Being surrounded by creative people makes it a very comforting atmosphere in which to work. I feel good about contributing to and supporting the idea of books as a traditional means of education."

—**Christina Renzi,** Book Compositor
Spark Publishing/Barnes & Noble

The Major Players

- **McGraw-Hill Education,** mcgraw-hill.com
  With headquarters in New York City and offices all over the world, McGraw-Hill serves a readership that includes early childhood, primary, secondary, post-secondary, and higher education, as well as professional development. It publishes books, online and multimedia tools, and e-books, covering everything from math to music to health to English as a Second Language (ESL). The huge media conglomerate McGraw-Hill Companies owns McGraw-Hill, as well as Standard &

Poor's, *BusinessWeek* magazine, Aviation Week Group, J. D. Power & Associates, McGraw-Hill Construction, and Platt.

- **Pearson Education,** pearsoned.com
  Pearson Education is part of the international media company Pearson, which also owns Penguin Group and Financial Times Group. Under the imprints of Prentice Hall, Addison Wesley, Allyn & Bacon, Alpha Books, and Adobe Press, Pearson Education publishes books on such subjects as business, technology, sciences, law, and humanities. Pearson's headquarters are in Upper Saddle River, New Jersey, though it has offices all over the world.

- **Houghton Mifflin,** hmco.com
  Headquartered in Boston, Massachusetts, Houghton Mifflin publishes textbooks, instructional technology, assessments, and other educational materials—in reading, language arts, math, social studies, science, and world languages—as well as reference books and fiction and nonfiction. Its imprints include American Heritage, McDougal Littell, Riverside, and Great Source. Some of its notable books include H. A. and Margret Ray's *Curious George*, Winston Churchill's *The Second World War,* and the *American Heritage Dictionary*.

- **Holt, Rinehart and Winston,** hrw.com
  Owned by Harcourt Classroom Education, Holt, Rinehart and Winston publishes secondary education (6–12) curriculum-based textbooks and reference materials in print, electronic, and online formats. Based in Austin, Texas, but with offices throughout the United States, Holt publishes materials that focus on language arts, science and health, social studies, world languages, and mathematics, as well as professional development resources.

66 I have worked at different types of houses, including a small university press, an educational press, and a commercial trade press. While there are job culture differences in each type of house, there was always one main goal: to put out a good book."

—**Karen Chaplin,** Assistant Editor
Penguin

2

WHAT KIND OF WORK COULD I DO?

FROM IDEA TO BOOKSHELF IN 8 EASY STEPS

How exactly does an idea become a book and ultimately make its way to your welcoming hands? Well, the process has more stages than you might think. Let's examine the life of a hypothetical book called *Satisfy Your Sweet Tooth: The Chocoholic's Weight-Loss Regimen,* by an unknown author named Jane.

1

Idea   Jane is a successful pastry chef in a small town. When one of her customers laments that he has to deprive himself of Jane's delicious pastries so he can lose a few pounds, Jane suddenly has an idea. Why not create and publish a weight-loss plan that allows people to eat chocolate? Not only would her bakery get publicity, but also her customers wouldn't feel guilty about eating her pastries. Sounds delicious. Jane doesn't know the first thing about getting a book published, so she finds a **literary agent,** who becomes Jane's representative to publishing houses. The agent helps Jane shape the idea into a **book proposal.** Together, they come up with the title *Satisfy Your Sweet Tooth: The Chocoholic's Weight-Loss Regimen.*

2

Acquisition   Jane's agent sends the *Sweet Tooth* proposal to editors at publishing houses that may be interested in publishing the book. When an editor likes the proposal, he presents it to a **pub board,** which includes other editors, the publisher, as well as sales representatives and members of the marketing/publicity and financial teams. When everyone on the team feels confident about Jane's potential book, the editor contacts the agent to tell her that he is interested in **acquiring** the book.

3

Bidding and Negotiation   Lucky for Jane, several publishing houses want to publish *Sweet Tooth*. To win the right to acquire it, the houses begin to **bid** by offering Jane a higher author's **advance,** or money paid to her up front, before the title has been published. This amount of money would be paid against her **royalties,** or the percentage of sales that Jane will receive once the book is published. (Once Jane earns out her advance, she'll begin to earn money from royalties.) When Jane gets an offer that she is pleased with, her agent then begins to negotiate her contract with the editor. They agree on a royalty rate (anywhere from 5 percent to 18 percent) and author's advance and determine **subsidiary rights,** such as rights to publish foreign translations, an audio version, or a series—perhaps Jane can write weight-loss plans for ice-cream lovers, cake addicts, pie eaters, and so on.

4

Manuscript   Jane then begins to write her book, working closely with her agent and editor to create a solid manuscript. Her editor helps her organize her writing, offers advice on style and content, and also **line edits,** or makes sure the writing is clear and means what Jane intended on a sentence-by-sentence level. When Jane and her editor are satisfied with the manuscript, the editor **transmits,** or gives, it to production.

5

Production   Production then sends the *Sweet Tooth* manuscript to a **copy editor,** who fine-tunes it by checking for correct grammar, punctuation, clarity, style, organization, and consistency. Jane reviews the copyedited manuscript, makes any necessary changes, and returns it to her editor, who also gives the manuscript a thorough reading. Meanwhile, the design team has been working closely with the editor and the sales and marketing/publicity teams to develop an interior design and cover for the book. Once the manuscript and design are final, production sends the manuscript to a **typesetter,** who lays out the pages as they will appear in the finished book. The typesetter then returns the typeset pages, or **page proofs,** back to the production team, who proofread them for errors and also show them to the editor, Jane, marketing/publicity, and sales for approval.

6

Marketing and Publicity   While *Sweet Tooth* is in production, the marketing/publicity team continues trying to create a buzz about the book. They conduct an analysis of sales data, demographic trends, and book reviews to plan and execute a publicity campaign. Working with Jane's schedule, they plan bookstore readings and signings, national and local television talk show appearances, call-in radio show interviews, newspaper and magazine interviews, and book parties attended by members of the press, celebrities, and other authors and publishing executives. Meanwhile, sales representatives all over the country have been talking to buyers at bookstores and libraries, trying to convince them to purchase the book.

7

Printing   Once the page proofs are final, production sends the files to a printer, who prints and binds the book.

8

Distribution   Sale representatives have been successful in their negotiations with buyers, and they place orders for *Sweet Tooth* through a distributor or wholesaler, who then sends the book to the stores and libraries that have ordered it. The book hits the bookstores' shelves and finally reaches the hands of interested chocoholics everywhere, including, perhaps, you.

As you can see, there's a lot more to creating a book than just having it written and printed. Writers and editors work with an extensive team to produce and sell a profitable, quality book that's perfect for its intended readers. The good news is that all these steps require tons of creative, energetic folks who love books. This chapter gives you all the info you need to discover more information about your perfect publishing job.

THE LAY OF THE LAND

But first, it's time to talk money. Chances are you don't want to be in publishing for the money. Right? We might as well tell you up front: If you want to make a lot of money, consider another career. For all but a few top-level execs, publishing isn't exactly a high-paying business. But you want to work with words, and that's the bottom line. Now you've just got to figure out where you belong. No matter where you find yourself, prepare to work hard for not a ton of money but to be continually stimulated and surrounded by myriad creative and like-minded individuals who love books just as much as you do.

66 Book publishing involves long hours and crummy pay at the start, but eventually you work short hours for great pay. And you never have to pay for a book."

—**Patrick Mulligan,** Assistant Editor, Gotham Books

The following list shows the departments of a publishing house. Directors oversee the staff in each department, and the publisher oversees everybody in the house. We'll go into more detail about the departments and jobs throughout this chapter.

- **Editorial Department**
- **Production and Manufacturing Department**
- **Design Department**
- **Sales Department**
- **Marketing/Publicity Department**

The publisher

The publisher is the head honcho of a publishing house or, in a big house, of an imprint. She ultimately decides which books get published and controls the purse strings and has final say on all budgets and finances. The publisher has a strong editorial, financial, and marketing/publicity background, and she's responsible for the overall direction—and profits!—of the house or imprint.

EDITORIAL

Have you ever thought, *Someone should write a book about this*? Do you constantly evaluate writing as you read, thinking, *This is good stuff*, or, *This writing stinks*? If you'd like to be the person who helps bring the words of unknown writers into the hands of hungry readers, you belong in editorial. By far the most glamorous department in publishing, editorial definitely has the most sought-after positions. But editorial isn't all about having long lunches with agents, taking meetings with big-name authors, and attending fancy-schmancy book parties. Editors work hard to find talented writers, negotiate with agents, come up with marketable book ideas, and produce quality manuscripts.

Personality Profile

- **You're creative, curious, and capable.** As an editor, you'll constantly be evaluating book ideas and proposals, looking for the

Book proposals include a summary of the book, an explanation of why the book should be published, who its readers would be, and why the author is the best person to write it; a detailed list of potential competition; an annotated chapter outline; and two sample chapters.

next big thing. You'll always have your antennae perked up for fertile markets and new talent. Depending on the house you work for, you'll scour literary journals for unheralded new writers, troll gossip blogs to see what—or whom—people are talking about, hang out at professional and scholarly conferences, or even channel surf during prime time to find out about the hot shows, stars, movies, and fashion trends. If you know a good idea when you see one or if you have the ability to transform something so-so into something *so great*, you've got *editor* written all over you.

- **You're addicted to words.** Editors work very closely with authors, helping them mold their writing into a perfect manuscript and sellable book. But this process takes time—a lot of time—and the manuscript goes through many, many revisions. As an editor, you'll be doing a lot of rewriting and revising, but you'll also be writing letters to your authors to help them rewrite and revise. If you love to read and write and if you have a stack of red pens in your closet, then editorial's the place for you.

66 Starting salaries are really low, and it takes a long time to get promoted. If you work in editorial, you can expect to spend at least five years answering someone else's phone and handling their correspondence while living on ramen noodles and spending your every waking hour (weekends too!) reading manuscripts. Is it worth it? Only if you really want to be an editor."

—**Julie Doughty,** Editor
Dutton

- **You're a smooth talker.** Editors spend a ton of time dealing with words on the page, natch, but they must also be able to communicate with real live human beings. You'll be helping authors write the perfect book, which sometimes means alternatively holding their hands as they struggle and sternly reminding them of deadlines and parameters. You'll need to articulate the author's vision of the book to the publisher, the design department, and the sales and marketing/publicity teams. Navigating between author and publisher can be tricky because not all authors care about the bottom line and not all publishers care about finely crafted prose. But the rewards are immense: A book that satisfies the author and the publisher is a beautiful thing to behold.

- **You can multitask with the best of them.** You may be rocking out to hip-hop music on your iPod while line editing a book about yoga, surfing for new literary agent contacts, and checking sales reports to see what types of books are flying off the virtual shelves. Responsible for acquiring, editing, and monitoring books through production, editors must be able to handle several projects, at different stages of the process, all at once. Think reviewing a book proposal, line editing a manuscript, reviewing pages, approving a cover, and giving an author a pep talk, throw in a ton of meetings and lunches, and you've got a good idea of the day-to-day job.

66 The actual editing does have its drawbacks. It is surprising how many writers, particularly in academia, cannot write. And as an editor, you have to be tactful in how you phrase your criticisms. Even though sometimes you wish the writer were sitting next to you so that you could slap him on the head and ask, 'What were you thinking when you wrote this?' "

—**Andrew Sylvester,** Associate Editor
SparkNotes

The Workplace

Working in editorial promises continual contact with creative and interesting authors (and maybe even celebrities!), and it also promises that you will eventually have an important say in which books get made and how they look. As a full editor, you'll someday be able to pursue whatever project strikes your fancy, though you will probably be somewhat limited by what subject areas will be most profitable for the publisher.

Expect to be busy, busy, busy. Not only will you read tons of manuscripts (which often means taking them home to read at night and on weekends), you'll also be placing your finger on the pulse of pop culture, sharpening your radar for the next bestseller or top-selling product. You'll meet with authors, scout out possible ideas by attending writers conferences, read magazines, and even rub elbows with celebrities, politicians, average Joes—anyone who has a story to tell. Sure, everyone has a story to tell and everyone wants to write a book, but the trick is knowing what everyone else wants to read.

How do editors decide which books to publish?

On the one hand, sometimes editors just have a "feeling" that a book has that "it" factor that will make it successful. But this intuition comes with time and experience.

On the other hand, there's actually a formula for what makes a book publishable. When an editor decides which ideas to pursue, he looks for potential books that meet some or all of the following criteria:

1. It provides an easy solution to a common problem.
2. It gives a sought-after answer to a popular question.
3. It offers new insight on a popular subject.
4. It's the next book in an already popular series.
5. It's written by an already successful author.
6. It's written by an expert on the topic.
7. It's written by or about a celebrity.
8. It's endorsed or praised by a celebrity or an expert.
9. It's written for a niche market that's easy to reach.
10. It's like no other book already published.
11. It's extremely well written, thoughtful, and all-around incredible.

Books don't always have to meet these criteria, though, in order to be published. Once in a while, a brave editor will take a chance—and perhaps even help to bring forth an unlikely bestseller. *The Memory Keeper's Daughter,* by Kim Edwards, had modest sales in hardcover (about 30,000 copies), only to skyrocket in paperback to the top of bestseller lists during the summer of 2006.

The Salaries

Salaries in editorial vary widely, depending on position and house. Smaller houses might pay less, but they allow you to do more, which means you can get promoted faster. Bigger houses have more glamour—and the competition for such jobs can be crazy! Getting hundreds of applications for just one editorial assistant position is not unheard of at places such as Random House and Penguin.

Top-level editorial job (editorial director, senior editor) salaries range from $80,000 to $166,000, middle-level (editor) from $40,000 to $75,000, and bottom-level (assistant editor, editorial assistant) from $28,000 to $40,000.

Think before you look

The job type you have, as well as the genre you work on, will determine your pathway up the career ladder. If your dream is to be an editor for literary fiction, working in production on romance novels won't get you there. While moving from design or production to editorial is possible, it's also difficult to switch departments, especially as you advance from entry-level positions. Think twice before taking a job you don't really want just to have a job. You'll likely have to backpedal eventually to get on the right track. So take the time to really think about where you want to be before you even start looking for jobs.

Prospects

Entry-level jobs in editorial have the toughest competition of all the departments in the industry. You'll need a liberal arts degree (think English, journalism, or history) for all but the most specialized houses. You'll also need to have a strong editorial and writing background (consider writing or editing publications in college or taking a class in editing or copyediting). Finally, you'll need a good dose of patience: Moving up the ladder takes a while, as in *years*. The possibility of moving up depends very much on the upper-level editors and how much of their work they decide to entrust to you. Some editors support their assistants' ambitions and allow them to acquire and edit books within the first couple of years. Some don't and won't—*ever*. On average, it takes about five or six years to see any significant upward movement in this department. A good gauge for how fast you're moving is to count how many books you're handling independently. The more books you have, the faster you're moving up.

Job Titles

Editors have a great many responsibilities and a great many titles. The general hierarchy goes from editorial assistant to assistant editor to associate editor to editor to senior editor to executive editor. Acquisitions and developmental editors tend to be senior or executive editors, meaning that they've been in the field for a while and know the industry inside and out. Associate and assistant editors tend to work on projects that have been acquired or developed by the more senior editors. We've organized the list below to give you a sense of the kinds of things editors do on a day-to-day basis.

- **Editorial Director/Editor in Chief**
  The editorial director or editor in chief is responsible for the overall editorial direction of the house or imprint. Ultimately, the decision about whether to publish a book rests with the publisher, but the editorial director has significant say. Basically, the editorial director runs the editorial department. She assigns responsibilities for implementing the editorial program, sets and approves its budgets, schedules and oversees its progress, and organizes the hierarchy, deciding who reports to whom and who handles which titles. She also is a liaison between the editorial and marketing/publicity departments, so the editorial director must not only have strong skills as an editor but also a thorough knowledge of market trends.

- **Acquisitions Editor**
  The acquisitions editor primarily solicits and evaluates manuscripts. He often finds promising manuscripts after reviewing book proposals, meeting with agents, or seeking out authors by attending conferences and networking. This editor often has a particular area of expertise, which he has honed over time, and he also has an extensive contact

list of literary agents, writers, established authors, and other media professionals. Like the publisher, the acquisitions editor has a keen sense of growing markets and spends much of his time reading magazines, newspapers, and trade journals to keep track of trends and competing titles. Once the acquisitions editor acquires a book, he works with the author and sometimes the agent to fine-tune the manuscript for quality while also developing and supporting the marketing/publicity effort. The acquisitions editor is usually fairly removed from the manuscript once it has been finalized and submitted to the production department for copyediting and typesetting.

- **Developmental Editor**
  The developmental editor literally develops books and series, from concept to bound book. Often, the developmental editor commissions a book—that is, she thinks of an idea and then hires a writer to write the specific book she has in mind—rather than acquiring a manuscript from an agent. Once the manuscript is in, she makes sure that it conforms to the original plan for the project, which might involve many back-and-forth discussions with the author about content and style. She also hires and manages freelance expert reviewers, who double-check that the content of the book meets industry standards. She plays an active role in the line editing and marketing of the book. Many publishing professionals choose to remain acquisitions or developmental editors rather than to move up and become editorial directors or editors in chief, because these top-level positions require more administrative and budgetary concerns and less hands-on book editing and developing.

- **Editor/Associate Editor/Assistant Editor**
  The editor works with production and monitors the process from manuscript to bound book. He has a hands-on role in shaping the manuscript into a marketable and readable product, working with the author on line editing, working with the designer on cover and interior design, and also writing jacket copy and copy for sales and marketing/publicity materials. The associate editor or assistant editor works

with the editor and authors on deadlines for submitting material. He also reads and recommends manuscripts to the editor, maintains direct contact with other departments during the production process, and handles many administrative duties, such as photocopying manuscripts for distribution.

The apprentice

The editorial department in particular and, to some degree, publishing in general operates on the apprentice system. When you're just starting out, you must apprentice yourself to a more senior member of your department. This person gives you feedback, pep talks, and projects. You must master a certain set of skills before you can even think about moving up. But being a good editor comes with time, experience, and practice. There's a reason why you can't simply major in "editing" or "publishing": These areas require extensive on-the-job training.

The Ground Floor

Becoming an editorial assistant is the first step toward becoming the mastermind behind which books get published. Everybody has to start somewhere, and most editors start as editorial assistants. You may find the job to be both demanding and menial, but it can also be very rewarding. It's probably the most highly sought-after entry-level position in the publishing industry, and honestly, it pretty much guarantees that you'll be overworked and underpaid. You'll spend much of your time reading the **slush pile** and answering correspondence. You'll also be writing reader's reports for the more promising manuscripts to give to the editor for review. To determine which manuscripts show potential, you'll check the competition and provide summaries of any similar books for comparison.

As an editorial assistant, you'll also handle the administrative and clerical work for the entire editorial department, including answering phones; taking minutes at editorial meetings; filing; photocopying; **trafficking,** or bringing, materials to other departments and managing the schedules of those materials; and mailing manuscripts and proofs to

The pile of unsolicited manuscripts that come in from agents and authors is known as the **slush pile.**

Literary agents

The intermediaries between writers and publishers, literary agents (or book scouts) have the all-too-important job of weeding out the bad manuscripts and shaping the manuscripts with potential into the books that publishers are looking for. If you think you have a knack for recognizing and promoting marketable talent, working at a literary agency might be perfect for you. Agents serve as an author's gateway to publishers. In turn, publishers count on literary agents to present them with marketable and extremely well-written book proposals or manuscripts that fit the publisher's needs. Most nonfiction proposals include a finished chapter or two, while fiction proposals usually include the entire manuscript.

Many publishers only accept manuscripts or proposals through agents, and many editors often go to agents with an editorial idea and then put the agents in charge of finding a writer for the job. A literary agent isn't just a writer's salesperson, however. The agent's work often begins with a writer's idea: The agent helps the writer to flesh it out and compose it into a book proposal, heavily edits the sample chapters or complete manuscript, and presents the book to various publishers. It's the agent's job to figure out which editors and houses might be right for the particular project the author has in mind. Once a publisher buys the book, the agent then negotiates the author's contract, typically receiving a 5–20 percent commission for the agenting services.

Entry-level positions at literary agencies, while competitive, are mostly administrative. Agencies get bombarded with manuscripts and proposals from aspiring writers, creating an overwhelming slush pile that needs to be sifted through. This duty often falls to the agents' assistants or agents-in-training, who must handle this heavy load on top of answering phones, sending out proposals, collating manuscripts, filing contracts, and processing royalty statements to no end.

Knowing how to recognize talent and saleable ideas takes time and experience. It helps to have both a solid writing background and knowledge of the publishing industry. You might begin your agenting career by working at a publishing house; this head start would give you valuable insider's knowledge. Advancement at a literary agency is completely dependent on persistence and ambition: If you constantly make connections with burgeoning writers and established editors at various houses, you'll work your way up. It's even better if you sell a manuscript that goes on to become a bestseller. As long as you make money for your agency, your author, and the publisher, you're golden.

authors for review. Your contact with authors will usually be limited to greeting them on the phone, although your boss might let you tag along to a lunch or book party. However, eventually an editor will let you begin to maintain direct contact with the author as her book is going through the production process. You'll be charged with making sure that everybody meets the various deadlines and that the author has ample time to review each stage. These responsibilities involve checking that the manuscripts are in the proper format for copyediting and typesetting, tracking and labeling art, and making comments on design and layout on behalf of the author.

Be prepared for a ton of reading!

You'll probably do much of your work-related reading on your own time, at home and on the weekends. Your job may seem overwhelming at first—balancing both the editorial and administrative work won't be easy. But the surest way to make your way up is to show initiative and demonstrate a thorough understanding of good writing and knowledge of what a reader wants. Finding the next bestseller won't hurt your chances of moving up either.

PRODUCTION AND MANUFACTURING

Do you love the sheer physicality of books? Are you a perfectionist who obsesses over every little detail? Do you like the idea of taking a manuscript and literally transforming it into that final polished product that ultimately reaches the hands of eager readers? How would you like to manage a crop of copy editors, proofreaders, fact-checkers, and indexers, all working from home as freelancers? The production and manufacturing team oversees the production process, making sure that the book includes all necessary materials; all deadlines are met; and the book meets high-quality standards in terms of style, grammar, and structure. Most publishing houses don't have the means in-house to typeset and print their books. Thus, houses hire freelance compositors, typesetters, and printers to do the job, and production manages the copy editors and proofreaders, who ensure that the books are perfect in every possible way. Production and manufacturing act as the liaison between the publishing house and the out-of-house staff who actually make the books.

Personality Profile

- **You're a grammar maven with a super-sharp eye.** You find yourself noticing—and getting annoyed by—typos on cereal boxes, takeout menus, movie posters, and classified ads. It takes a trained and careful eye to be able to catch errors and inconsistencies, and some people have more of a knack for this than others. Your most important job in production is to prevent errors in the finished book. This means making sure that there are no typos and misspellings, that all illustrations and page numbers are in the right place, and that the book is generally in high-quality, publishable shape before printing, even down to the size of the book (known as its **trim size**) and the kind of paper it's printed on.

- **You like to tell people what to do and when to do it.** Countless elements—contributed by the author, editor, designer, artists, and many freelancers, such as copy editors, fact-checkers, proofreaders, and indexers—go into making a book. The production and manufacturing department must make sure that all components come together in an organized fashion and that deadlines are met to guarantee the book publishes on time. They often have to keep track of several books at once, each of which is on a much different schedule, has different elements, and is at a different stage of the process.

- **You love the smell, feel, and look of books.** You like the size of the pages, the typeface, and the cloth cover. You're attracted to books at a bookstore not because of the title but because they feel good when you hold them. Not only that, but you've been designing the family Christmas letter since you were 10, and you're constantly changing the fonts in your IM chat windows, so you know a little about typography and laying out pages. You'll be working very closely with the designers and communicating with the typesetter to implement the designers' instructions, so you'll need to know—and love—everything about the books' physical makeup.

Don't leave your galley in the gutter

Here's a list of some of the key terms used by the production and manufacturing department:

- **bleeds:** To ensure that color extends all the way to the edge of a page, a printer will "bleed" the color by printing over the *crop lines*.

- **crop lines:** The lines printed on a page or proof that indicate where the pages will be cut by the printer.

- **dummy:** A fake book with blank pages and cover produced by the printer so that the editorial, art, and sales and marketing/publicity departments can see how the book will actually look and feel once it's published.

- **galley:** Page proofs of part or all of a manuscript that get sent to critics in the hopes that they will choose to review the book.

- **gutters:** The space between the printed text and physical edge of the page.

- **kerning:** The space between letters.

- **print run:** The number of books to be printed.

- **spine:** The part of the book that faces out when it's shelved.

- **trim size:** The physical measurements of the book. The trim size of *Spark Your Career in Book Publishing* is 7.5×9.125.

❝ I love being busy and organizing things and looking for better ways to accomplish things. I really enjoy working for a smaller company because it's easier to get into areas that aren't technically in your job description. I got into book publishing because I wanted to work on non-advertising-driven publications (i.e., not magazines or newspapers) and to work on things I might actually read."

—**Andrea Colvin,** Executive Managing Editor
Harry N. Abrams

The Workplace

In production and manufacturing, everything that was previously just an idea becomes realized, put together, polished, and printed. Jobs in this department involve a lot of juggling and sticking to deadlines, and it may seem overwhelming to keep track of every book—where it is in the process, whether it's sticking to the budget, what's missing, and which things still need to get done. Here, though, you get the best exposure to the complicated process of creating a book. You also have the pleasure of being hands-on in that process without having to deal with sometimes very demanding (and annoying) authors or being responsible for the content.

Despite tireless efforts to implement schedules, deadlines are often—well, usually—not met. Unfortunately, when this happens, the production and manufacturing department has to pick up the slack and shave time off of the schedule. You may spend much of your time trafficking materials and waiting for them to be brought back to you after the right people have reviewed them. But you're not going to be watching the clock. While waiting, you'll be working on schedules, crunching numbers to determine production costs, maintaining contact with typesetters and printers to make sure changes are getting made, and working with design and editorial to make sure that all the material is included in the book that needs to be. This material includes any illustrations, charts, **front matter,** and **back matter.**

front matter:
Copyright page, title page, prologue, introduction.

back matter:
Epilogue, appendices, notes, bibliography, index.

The Salaries

Generally, production and manufacturing jobs pay better than editorial jobs. Top-level production and manufacturing job (director of production and manufacturing, managing editor) salaries range from $55,000 to $100,000, middle-level (production supervisor, production editor) from $40,000 to $66,000, and bottom-level (assistant production editor, production assistant) from $28,000 to $40,000.

Prospects

Prospects for getting an entry-level job in production and manufacturing are much easier than for other departments. Although it's a highly specialized department that's integral to the publishing process, fewer newbies seem to pursue this track compared to editorial, marketing/publicity, or sales. To get a job, you'll likely be tested on your eye for detail and knowledge of grammar by taking a copyediting and proofreading test, and you'll need to have experience in project management. Moving up in production and manufacturing happens much faster than it does in editorial, and the promotion process is very straightforward by comparison. In editorial, your upward mobility depends on the support of the editor you work for, but in production and manufacturing, you just have to show increased skills in project management, estimating costs and planning budgets, and copyediting and proofreading. Now, sharpening your expertise will take time, of course, and you'll also have to gain experience working on several types of books to show you can handle a variety of projects. The advantage, though, is that the pathway for moving up is clear-cut, whereas it might be more ambiguous in other departments.

Job Titles

- **Director of Production and Manufacturing**
  The director determines the specifications and production processes, establishing the overall production department plans and roles. He procures the raw materials for printing the books by maintaining relationships with suppliers and ensuring that they meet their obligations to the publishing house for quality, cost, and schedule. The director also manages most of the company's budget, as well as its technology assets, and negotiates some of the company's largest contracts, such as those with typesetters, printers, and distributors.

- **Managing Editor**
  The managing editor is the liaison between production and editorial and usually oversees a sub-department within the larger production and manufacturing department known as **managing editorial** or **production editorial.** She acts as the central source of information for all other departments. Her other tasks include developing procedures for controlling the flow from manuscript to bound book; coordinating the progress of scheduling and production; overseeing the hiring of freelance copy editors, proofreaders, and indexers; and

establishing editorial guidelines. The managing editor also assists in preparing the publisher's budget and publication schedule, which contains all pertinent information for each book, including the publication month and on-sale date, author, title, ISBN, dimensions, and U.S. and Canadian prices.

Copyediting vs. proofreading

Copyediting involves checking a manuscript for consistency and correctness in style, grammar, and punctuation. A copy editor creates a **style sheet** for the manuscript, which lists the spellings of words and proper nouns that the author uses frequently, as well as gives notes on the author's style of writing. A copy editor also often suggests changes to the author for purposes of clarity, and he often **fact-checks,** or does research to check that all facts (people, places, dates, events, etc.) are correct (this usually only applies to nonfiction).

Proofreading involves checking for errors once the manuscript has been **typeset,** or laid out as the final book. A proofreader (also known as a proofer) checks that the text matches what was in the manuscript, rechecks for consistency and correctness in grammar and punctuation (using the copy editor's style sheet as a guide), and also checks that all major components—chapters, page numbers, illustrations, headings—are in the right place.

- **Production Supervisor**

  While the managing editor supervises the production of the book's content, the production supervisor manages the creation of the actual book. He develops and manages production schedules and budgets. He also secures estimates based on project specifications and selects vendors based on these estimates and consults with editors on specifications for paper, cloth, binding, and typography. The production supervisor, along with the managing editor, tracks and monitors all stages of production to ensure quality, accuracy, and timeliness of the final bound book.

- **Production Coordinator**

  The production coordinator has the most direct contact with the production editors in managing editorial as well as with the design department. With a good understanding of production planning and the ability to work under tight deadlines, she schedules and traffics work among in-house departments and outside vendors. The production coordinator must have excellent troubleshooting and quality-control skills, as well as be familiar with desktop publishing. Good communication skills are essential too because production coordinators are the main contact for the editorial and manufacturing departments and for out-of-house production services.

- **Senior Production Editor**

  The senior production editor handles manuscripts once they are submitted from the editorial department. He copyedits—or hires a freelance copy editor—to check the manuscript for style, consistency, spelling, grammar, and punctuation. He maintains direct contact with the editors in order to resolve any issues involving inconsistencies in style and information. Once the manuscript is typeset, the senior production editor proofreads—or hires a freelance proofreader—to check the page proofs for errors. In addition to monitoring the production process of the books' interiors, the senior production editor proofreads the covers, jackets, and marketing/publicity materials for the books. The senior production editor must also keep track of the progress of all titles and prepare status reports for the managing editor.

> ### A note on style
>
> Production people must be experts on grammar but must also have a sense of the nuances of every author's style and what each author intends to accomplish with his or her writing. This job requires a great deal of tact, for it is the production editor's responsibility to find common ground between the **house style**—the publisher's preferences for spelling, grammar, punctuation, and typography—and the author's style.

- **Production Editor/Associate Production Editor**

  The production editor has much of the same responsibility as the senior production editor but handles fewer books and handles them under the supervision of both the managing editor and the senior production editor. The production editor also assists the senior production editor in hiring freelancers and proofreading covers, jackets, and marketing/publicity materials. Once the manuscript has been typeset, reviewed by the author, and proofread, the production editor collates all the corrections onto one master set of **page proofs,** or the complete set of typeset pages, and submits the proofs to production so that the corrections can be made. She also makes sure all materials are received on time from the authors and keeps track of any missing materials throughout the process.

66 I love reading all the teen girl novels from start to finish, seeing the covers come together. I also love that [my job as production editor] allows me to work so independently. I dislike checking blues, because it's tedious and monotonous, but it has to get done!"

—**Melinda Weigel,** Production Editor
HarperCollins Children's Books

The Ground Floor

Ready for a juggling act? Production and manufacturing actually make the books, so there's always a lot happening—and you'll be at the center of it all. Okay, so you might be busy handling multiple projects simultaneously, but you'll always be in the know about what's going on with every book in the process. There are two possible ground-floor positions, both of which involve a great deal of administrative work and trafficking.

If your goal is to eventually become a managing editor, becoming an assistant production editor/managing editorial assistant is a good place to start. You'll be the managing editor's go-to guy (or gal) when it comes to keeping track of all the books, helping to continually update the in-house publishing schedule. You'll also be assisting the production editors by copying manuscripts and page proofs and trafficking them to other departments for approval; sending out manuscripts and page proofs to freelance copy editors, proofreaders, and indexers; and routing covers throughout all departments for approval. You may also take part in proofreading page proofs and covers, as well as copyediting front matter, back matter, flap copy, and marketing/publicity materials. You've got to love details and schedules, and you can't have any qualms about (subtly) nagging other departments to meet deadlines once in a while.

The other possible position is a production assistant. As a production assistant, you'll support the production coordinator in the development of the schedule and help keep the production schedule up-to-date. Expect to spend a lot of time on the phone, on email, and at a fax machine. You'll have to be in constant contact with outside vendors, as well as with all in-house departments, to make sure that last-minute changes are made to page proofs in order for the book to be printed on time. But since you're the last line of communication between the publishing house and the team that actually prints the book, your role is crucial.

❝ Choose what type of position suits your personality. There are editorial departments and there are production departments. If you are creative and like to travel, go editorial. If you like words for the sake of words, go production."

—**Emerson John Probst,** Senior Editor
Marketplace Books

DESIGN

Book covers often determine whether a customer picks up a book—and buys it—or whether a customer walks right on by. So the book cover design is critical, and some cover designers become quite famous in the field for creating attractive covers that not only grab readers but also convey the message of the book. The design department creates the face and "look" of every book, both by designing the cover and interior and by producing most marketing, publicity, and advertising materials. Working very closely with editorial and marketing/publicity to make sure their ideas are properly artistically realized, the design team plays a huge role in the book production process.

Personality Profile

- **You judge a book by its cover.** You marvel at how the book's title jumps out at you, how it's embossed and juxtaposed over the image just so. When you finish a book, you look at the cover again, and you feel impressed by how well the design matched the storyline. A book's design must both effectively communicate the concept of the book's content and compel a reader to pick it up and buy it. If you have artistic vision and know how to shape it toward the very specific purposes of a book, you'll dig design.

- **You wouldn't be caught dead in a twinset and pencil skirt.** You're artsy and proud of it. Along with the author, you're the creative force behind the book. You're all about the art, and that's the way you like it. Let someone else worry about content and commas, schedules and salability. To you, the book itself is a thing of beauty. You love the challenge of interpreting the author's words and themes into a fitting design.

- **You know QuarkXPress and InDesign better than the back of your hand, and you'd never, ever dream of working on a PC.** You dream everything in pixels, and you're a whiz at using Photoshop to make blemishes disappear. Maybe you've even done layout for the college yearbook or your college dorm's weekly newsletter. Not only are you an artist, but you're also a graphic designer who knows all the layout programs and can work a Mac like nobody's business. You've got the artistic vision and the computer savvy required for book design. The rest of the design department will expect you to know these computer programs before getting the job, so don't anticipate that kind of on-the-job training. You don't have to be an expert in QuarkXPress or InDesign, but you should definitely know the basics before applying.

The Workplace

This is where the magic happens. We all know how important the design is, and here's where it's born. In particular, the design department regularly holds cover meetings, in which the designers discuss concepts for the covers with the editor, marketing/publicity and sales folks, the editorial director, and the publisher. A typical workday for a designer depends on the complexity of the types of books her imprint or press publishes. Regardless, expect a high degree of creative energy, somewhat restricted by the need to meet deadlines.

Since cover designs are so crucial in terms of marketing/publicity and interior designs take more time and are often more complex, often two different designers work separately on the cover and interior of the same book. When it comes to designing the interior, the design department creates sample page layouts based on the editorial concept and, usually, a few representative chapters. Once the editorial and marketing/publicity departments approve these layouts and covers, the designer instructs the typesetter on how to implement this design using the sample layouts and files. On more complex books, the designer will often hire freelance artists and designers to create cover and interior designs. This is often the case for books that are highly illustrated, such as photography books or children's books.

The Salaries

Top-level design job (creative or art director) salaries range from $75,000 to $150,000, middle-level (designer) from $40,000 to $100,000, and bottom-level (design assistant) from $28,000 to $40,000.

Prospects

Positions in the design department are often as competitive to get as those in the editorial department. In fact, many publishing houses don't even have entry-level design positions. To be hired as a book designer, you'll need to have a very strong portfolio and some background in freelance book design or graphic design. Many people also get their foot in the door by starting out in the production and manufacturing department, then switching over to design when a position opens up. Once there, though, you'll have an excellent chance of gaining more responsibility and bigger projects.

Job Titles

- **Creative Director/Art Director**

  The creative director, who often has a particular style that she is known for (like the brilliantly packaged Workman covers or classic-looking Knopf covers), establishes the overall artistic guidelines and quality-control standards for the publisher, maintaining these standards based on an understanding of the market and creative trends. He runs the design department and oversees all aspects of the design process from the original concept to the bound book. The creative director is responsible for understanding the editorial vision and communicating this vision to in-house and freelance designers. He assigns projects to designers and commissions freelance artists, illustrators, and photographers to create all the design elements for the book. Finally, the creative director also works with the marketing/publicity department to either create or oversee the creation of the marketing and publicity materials for the books published by the house.

- **Artist/Designer/Junior Designer**

  The book designer designs all elements of the book, including the cover or jacket, page layouts, title page, chapter openers, endpapers, and spine—all according to a design theme that meets the requirements of editorial, marketing/publicity, and production. Depending on the size of the publishing house, different people design the cover and the interior of a particular book. The designer decides typefaces for the text on the inside as well as the **display type,** or the typeface for the title, chapter openers, and other decorative text. She works with production and manufacturing to determine which materials to use for printing and what special elements to include, such as cover embossing and interior colors. She commissions photographers and artists for cover and interior images and illustrations and cleans up and color-corrects photos and artwork with graphic design software.

When designing a book, designers must create **templates,** or a standard design. A designer's role is especially crucial in developing children's books (pairing up a good author-illustrator team) and textbooks (filled with color photographs and illustrations, timelines, charts, and graphs). Mass-market paperbacks, however, require little design work, since the designer is limited by the small size of the books.

The parts of a book

A designer's artistic vision isn't just applied to the front cover of a book, even though that's the most important part. Many other parts of a book often need some careful thought in terms of design.

- The **back cover** of a hardcover book usually contains an excerpt from the book or praise for the book written by other authors, celebrities, or experts on the book's topic. Back covers of paperbacks have a summary of the book, as well as a brief biography of the author.

- The **front flap** of a hardcover book gives a summary of the book.

- The **back flap** of a hardcover book gives a short biography of the author.

- The **spine** contains the book title, the author's name, and the logo of the imprint or publisher.

- **Endpapers** bind the hard cover to the bound interior pages and are often made of heavier stock. They usually match the book design in color and sometimes have a special design relating to the book's concept.

- **Chapter openers** are always uniform within a book, using the same typeface and design elements throughout. Chapter openers often also include a quotation (known as an **epigraph**). The first word of the chapter's first line sometimes appears in a fancy typeface or in a much bigger font known as a **drop cap.**

- **Running heads** and **feet** are text at the top or bottom of every page that contain the name of the book, the name of the author, or the name of the chapter.

- Like the spine, the **title page,** which appears close to the beginning of the book, shows the book title, the author name, and the logo of the imprint or publisher.

The Ground Floor

Your first step toward becoming a book designer is becoming a design assistant if possible. Some houses don't have design assistants, in which case you might start as a junior designer. As a design assistant, you'll provide administrative help to the creative director and the designers. You'll be trafficking materials through other departments, as well as helping the designers keep track of their various projects. Once a book has already begun the production process, you'll step in to make sure the designer's instructions were followed, in particular that the page proofs match the sample page layouts the designer provided.

You may also be entrusted to handle designing books based on templates that the designers have already provided, or you may get to design some smaller elements of the book once the cover design and major interior elements are complete. Perhaps you'll get a chance to do some work on the marketing/publicity materials. Much like an editorial assistant, whether you move up the ladder quickly largely depends on how many books your supervisor allows you to handle independently.

MARKETING AND PUBLICITY

Without marketing and publicity, great books with awesome designs would languish and slowly die on bookstore shelves. The marketing and publicity department makes sure that people not only know about certain books but also get excited about buying them. This department functions as the publishing company's—and the author's—gateway to the potential consumer. For this very reason, marketing and publicity people offer input on every decision, from the initial concept of the book down to the title and cover design. They also work with editorial to decide which audiences they should aim toward via advertising and publicity, and they make these decisions based on careful analysis of sales results of past competitive titles. Then they launch a publicity campaign, making sure that the authors and their books get as much press coverage as possible. This involves planning book parties, sending out advance copies for book reviews, and arranging interviews, book signings, and author appearances.

Marketing concerns anything designed to reach a book's intended audience; **publicity** involves anything designed to generate buzz in the culture at large.

Personality Profile

- **You can spot market trends.** You read everything from the *New Yorker* to *InStyle* to *Atlantic Monthly* to *Us Weekly,* all while watching *Extra* and PBS (plus *The Daily Show* during commercials). You're ridiculously up-to-date on popular culture. Knowing who and what is hot now and in the near future is essential to marketing and publicizing books. You've got to know how to find your readers by knowing who they are, what they watch, what they read, what they eat, what they like, and where they shop.

The buzz on creating a buzz—creatively

A continual challenge for marketing and publicity is finding unique ways to reach their readers. Take Penguin, for example, which has joined forces with BzzAgent, a national company that creates a buzz about its clients' products just by word of mouth. BzzAgent's army of "buzzers" place themselves among their target market and chat up the book: It worked for *The Art of Shen Ku,* by Zeek. BzzAgent helped to revive the sales after the book had gathered dust for several years. HarperCollins has also jumped on the viral marketing/publicity bandwagon. Meg Cabot, whose *The Princess Diaries* has become highly successful among preteens, has a website that includes a blog, animated clips, and a feature that sends text messages to fans who opt to receive them. Harper's blog CruelestMonth.com features the publisher's poets, and Knopf sends out a poem-of-the-day e-mail and also publishes a podcast with poetry readings of Knopf popular authors. Just about anything goes as long as it helps sell books.

- **You love being in the spotlight—or helping someone else to be.** You're an enthusiastic people person. You love working with people and getting them excited about something, and you get excited very easily yourself. If your enthusiasm is contagious, you'll be an asset to the marketing/publicity department. As a publicist or marketing specialist, you'll be working to make sure the author gets a lot of attention, and you may be in the flash of the camera lens right alongside him or her. Say "cheese."

- **You've got style and flair to spare, baby.** You're quite the host, if you do say so yourself. In order to make sure the author gets a great deal of media attention, you'll have to plan a plethora of events, such as book launch parties, book signings, and author interviews and appearances. Event planning requires a certain amount of stylish organization. You'll have to work with the schedules of the author and the various media and keep everybody involved excited about the event. And what's not to be excited about? This job combines fame, fortune, and books.

The Workplace

A book won't become successful if the public has no idea it exists. The main job of the marketing and publicity department is to generate a buzz about each and every book published by the house. The media are saturated, so the marketing and publicity department must work tirelessly to somehow get the attention of as many magazines, newspapers, radio stations, blogs, and television talk shows as possible. Even the smallest amount of exposure could boost a book's sales tremendously, beyond the author's **platform.**

Working in marketing and publicity is very exciting because this department ensures that a book travels from the publishing house to the consumer. You'll really get to know the books your company publishes, and, most of all, you'll discover exactly what about them attracts readers. You'll use your keen insight into pop culture to figure out how to get people excited about a book, and you'll plan advertising campaigns and author events. Particularly in a big commercial publishing house, the work of the marketing and publicity department can make or break the sales of a book. Expect to be in constant communication with nearly all departments—editorial, production and manufacturing, design, and sales—while also maintaining frequent communication with all types of media and sales outlets. Working in marketing/publicity requires a high level of organization, creativity, and number-savvy, so be prepared to hone these very valuable skills.

An author's **platform** is his or her ready-made, built-in audience. For example, Oprah's platform for her books and magazines is the people who watch her television show. Marketing and publicity departments often work with editorial to develop an author's platform.

The Salaries

Top-level marketing and publicity jobs (marketing/publicity director) salaries range from $70,000 to $158,000, middle-level (publicist) from $40,000 to $90,000, and bottom-level (marketing assistant, publicity assistant) from $28,000 to $36,000.

Prospects

Entry-level jobs in marketing and publicity aren't as available as those in production, but they're definitely less competitive to get than those in editorial or design. Whether you move up in marketing and publicity depends on your motivation, your knowledge of market trends, your contacts in the business, and, naturally, whether your marketing/publicity efforts help sales. If you show your supervisor that you not only know the inside scoop on which show is the latest teen hit and why but also know exactly how to use your inside knowledge to sell a YA novel, you'll be more likely to move up quickly. Media contacts count too, so you'll need to know everyone who's anyone to get an author media attention.

Job Titles

- **Marketing/Publicity Director**

  The marketing/publicity director develops marketing/publicity objectives, policies, and strategies for each book and market. He has the very important and daunting responsibility of identifying the marketing/publicity capability of the publisher's books, spotting trends, and integrating market research and information about product development. The marketing/publicity director gives his approval at every stage of the process, from book concept to design to the production process to the planning and implementation of promotion and publicity campaigns. He also forecasts and manages sales budgets and works directly with promotion, publicity, and sales.

- **Promotion Manager**

  The promotion manager schedules advertising, direct mail, exhibits, and promotional activities. She also maintains contact with all media outlets, reviews industry reports, and consults on catalogs, in-store displays, and all sales and marketing/publicity tools. The promotion manager works directly with the editorial and marketing/publicity directors to coordinate promotional, publicity, and marketing activities.

The average promotion period for most books is just 60 days. To help extend that tiny window, many authors, and even some houses, hire freelance publicists to help generate buzz indefinitely.

How does the marketing/publicity team figure out how to reach a book's market?

When determining a marketing/publicity plan for a book, the team might ask themselves a number of questions.

1. **Does the subject of the book revolve around a certain holiday or time of year?** A book about applying to colleges, for example, would get its audience's attention most if it were published in the fall. A book about Yao Ming would be published at the beginning of basketball season.

2. **Does the book cater to a specific market that's easy to find?** A book about home decor, for example, would be strategically placed at Home Depot or Bed, Bath and Beyond.

3. **Is the author of the book a major selling point?** If of-the-moment actress Sara Superstarlet is the author, for example, her photograph would surely be placed boldly on the cover of the book and news of her book would be spread via fan sites and gossip magazines. If the author has published previous successful books but has an unrecognizable face, her name would likely appear in large print on the front—maybe even bigger than the title.

4. **Is the author an expert who can speak eloquently on her expertise?** Someone such as Dr. Phil, for example, who is not only a published author but also an experienced speaker, would go on an extensive speaking tour organized by the publisher's publicity team. But an author who's a brilliant writer but not a great speaker probably would not get such an extensive tour.

5. **Can the book's topic be molded for different markets?** A book on careers, for example, could be targeted toward recent college graduates but also toward older professionals looking to change careers or younger students looking to get a jump on their futures. In order to hit all markets, then, the marketing/publicity team would create different promotional and advertising materials to cater to these very different markets.

- **Marketing Manager**

  The marketing manager creates **marketing campaigns,** or strategies for reaching a book's intended audience, and determines a book's **sales channels,** or the best places for a book to be sold. He works directly with salespeople, providing them with catalogs and other promotional materials to give to booksellers to get them excited about upcoming titles and to get their feedback about improving or repackaging any backlist titles.

- **Publicity Manager**

  The publicity manager oversees the publicists' planning of **publicity campaigns,** or series of events held to create a buzz about an author or a book. She also has established relationships with key media outlets and book reviewers, ensuring that books get exposure through author interviews, feature articles, and book reviews. The publicity manager prepares press releases and stories on authors and their books and distributes them to newspapers, magazines, television talk show producers, and radio shows. With the help of the publicists, the publicity manager plans authors' parties, organizes author tours, and maintains clippings files of reviews and other press coverage given to books and authors.

- **Senior Publicist/Publicist**

  Each publicist is assigned several books by the publicity manager and is in charge of each book's publicity campaign. Publicists generate a buzz about the book even before it's published to ensure that there will be strong reader interest once the book hits the shelves. They also send ARCs to book reviewers at newspapers and magazines, radio stations, television talk shows, and websites. Finally, publicists create **press kits,** which contain pertinent information about the book, the author, and any selling points that would encourage members of the press to give the book exposure.

The **advance reader's copy (ARC),** which is an uncopyedited galley of the book sent to bookstores, book reviewers, other authors, and even celebrities, is a key publicity tool created by the marketing and publicity department. Positive book reviews and testimonials are then used on publicity materials and on the book cover.

66 As a publicist, I like to start off my morning going over the papers—
you might catch one of your authors in a piece you weren't expecting or
you might get ideas for future pitches. It's also good to know what types of
stories different reporters are working on—learning their 'beats' is easiest
when you read a paper day in and day out."

—**Colleen Schwartz,** Senior Publicist
St. Martin's Press

The Ground Floor

Because the marketing and publicity department is where the book begins
its journey toward the hands of eager readers, expect to be at the beck and
call of not only your boss but also of authors, journalists, editors, agents, and
publicists. Marketing and publicity help everyone outside of the publishing
house find out about the hot titles and authors, so you'll need to be on your
toes, always ready to send people whatever information they need right
when they need it or to talk about your house's titles on the fly. There are two
possible ground-floor positions, both of which involve a great deal of mailing
and administrative work: marketing assistant and publicity assistant.

As a marketing assistant, you'll be assisting the go-to person for all
information regarding the markets for a certain book. You'll maintain
databases, mailing lists, and sales records; distribute advance review copies of books; and assist in preparing catalogs and promotional materials.
You'll also help the marketing/publicity team keep track of market trends
by monitoring media coverage of backlist and front-list titles. You'll often
assist in market research by conducting surveys or interviewing consumers one-on-one and ultimately help to compile all the research results for
analysis. A major part of your job will be preparing and sending out mailings, which contain sales catalogs, ARCs, and other promotional materials.
These mailings are bulky since various media outlets and booksellers need
to be reached, so it takes a great deal of organization to keep track of them
and make sure everyone gets what they need.

As a publicity assistant, much like the marketing assistant, you'll spend much of your time doing mailings, though you'll be mailing press kits (personalized to each book and its author) to members of the media to encourage them to hold events or provide press coverage for authors and their books. You'll assist the publicists in preparing these press kits for each book, and you'll also make travel and lodging arrangements for authors who are going on tour. Plus, you'll help plan author events and interviews. Much like an editorial assistant, you may be lucky enough to have direct contact with the author, and you might even get to attend, hold, and host author events.

SALES

Once the marketing/publicity department has determined a book's intended audience and after the promotion and publicity have created a buzz, the sales team finally sells the books. The sales team is made up primarily of sales representatives all over the United States whose aim is not to sell directly to consumers but rather to the middlemen in three major markets: libraries, bookstores and retailers, and colleges.

Personality Profile

- **You could sell a cake to a baker or the Brooklyn Bridge to a New Yorker.** People in sales must be able to sell anything to anyone. They're great talkers who exude confidence without being annoying or arrogant. If you can charm your way into a customer's heart, then you'll be a natural in sales.

- **You love doing your own thing on your own time.** You want to work in publishing but hate the idea of sitting at a desk for eight hours a day reading or designing. You value your personal independence, but you're responsible enough to get things done without someone crowding you with suggestions or menial tasks. You know how to manage your time and your projects.

General retailers have become the largest and most important domestic channel of book distribution. Non-bookstore retail establishments, such as discount stores like Wal-Mart, have captured most of book sales, so sales teams definitely focus on these outlets.

- **You've got major wanderlust.** Working in sales involves a fair amount of traveling. That means you get to see a lot of places, but it also means that you might have some long hours away from your family and friends. You may be working on your own time, but traveling sometimes means your workday could last as long as 12 hours as you get from place to place.

- **You love to talk.** Look up *extrovert* in the dictionary, and there you are. You know how to command attention and talk articulately in any situation. You're persuasive and a brilliant negotiator. You have that rare skill of diplomacy: You know how to please your publisher *and* your customer. You know exactly what books your publisher wants to sell, and you also know which bookstores can and want to sell them.

- **Making money makes you happy.** If you're looking for a job in publishing where your hard work will pay off fast—*literally*—this is it. You can really make a lot in sales if you put in the effort and have the skills, since you earn more if you sell more.

The Workplace

If your reasons for working in publishing were to read and get excited about as many books as possible, you'll love it in the sales department. You've got one goal in sales: to sell books. You'll spend your days (and sometimes your nights) persuading bookstores and buyers to stock the titles published by your house. You'll need to have a thorough understanding of every book, as well as what kinds of books your clients (the booksellers, retailers, and distributors) can sell. But you won't just have to get to know every book and author of the season inside and out—you'll also have to be excited about every one. Sales pitches need to be carefully tailored to each bookseller, retailer, or distributor in order to be effective. You wouldn't want to pitch a book about the challenges of living cheaply in an expensive urban environment, for example, to a bookseller in a small town in Kansas. Know thy books, and know thy customers.

Sales representatives get assigned one of three different markets—libraries, bookstores, and colleges—depending on the types of books the publisher sells.

The Salaries

The representatives' major sales tool is the publisher's seasonal **catalog.**

Top-level sales job (sales director) salaries range from $170,000 to $300,000, middle-level (sales representative) from $39,000 to $100,000, and bottom-level (sales assistant) around $30,000. In addition to their annual, or **base,** salary, many sales representatives earn a commission, which, of course, drives them to make as many sales as possible.

Prospects

The prospects for getting an entry-level job in sales are fairly competitive, especially if you have no experience in sales. The possibility of moving up in the sales department depends on your ability to sell, sell, sell. The more you sell, the faster you move up—it's as simple as that. Make money for your company, and you'll be on your way to the corner office super-fast.

Special sales

In addition to finding creative ways to generate publicity about their books, publishing companies also have a **special sales** department devoted to focusing on nontraditional book markets, such as convenience stores, video stores, health food stores, computer stores, catalogs, and online retailers. Simon & Schuster, for example, partnered with gift packagers to reformat paperback titles, which were stuffed into 5.8 million Cheerios boxes as part of General Mills' literacy program. Harcourt published a book on the Apollo space program and sold it not just to book retailers but also to the Johnson Space Center and NASA museums. Another example? They sold *The Encyclopedia of Surfing* in surf shops.

Job Titles

- **Sales Director**
  The sales director oversees the entire sales force. He recruits, trains, and motivates the sales representatives; conducts sales meetings; and assigns territories. He develops budgets and **forecasts,** introduces the new books to the sales representatives, and compiles field reports for analysis. The sales director, along with the marketing, promotion, and publicity

forecasts: Predictions as to how many books will sell.

managers, also influences the creation of book jackets and promotional materials, and he works with marketing/publicity in the creation of the sales catalog. Finally, he maintains consistent contact with major bookstore chains, distributors, and other important sales outlets.

- **Regional Sales Manager**
  The regional sales manager supervises the sales representatives within a particular region, such as the southwestern United States, providing sales support and service to bookstores and other sales outlets within that region. She also travels to the region as the representative of the publishing house.

- **Sales Representative**
  The sales representative visits bookstores, libraries, schools, and colleges to take orders from seasonal sales catalogs. A regional sales manager assigns her to cover a particular territory, such as Texas, and he makes sure to inform every customer within that territory of the publisher's front-list titles. In order to become well versed in these titles, the sales rep attends seasonal sales meetings, where she gets the sales materials, including the sales catalog, order forms, promotional materials, and sales kits, which include a mock-up of every book cover and details about each book. The sales rep then travels to customers, pitching to book buyers and at trade shows and conferences. Larger publishers have their own house reps, who are salaried and whose expenses are paid, while smaller publishers hire independent reps on commission.
  The sales rep also has the very important responsibility of representing the publishing company to the wholesale-buying market. She becomes the face of the publisher, as well as its eyes and ears, regularly reporting back from the "field" on sales data and retail trends. In turn, analysis of those trends often drives the editorial development process.

The Ground Floor

If you'd rather sell books than edit, make, or design them, then you should head to sales (*duh*!). Unfortunately, you can't start out in the "field" at the beginning, but there are a couple of ways to get your foot in the door.

One ground floor position is a sales assistant. As a sales assistant, you'll provide in-house support for the sales managers and the sales reps out in the field. You'll send out sales materials to the sales reps and compile and distribute sales reports to managers. This job requires strong data entry and presentation skills.

Another possible entry-level position in sales is a telemarketing sales rep. Working in telemarketing involves taking catalog orders over the phone or Internet, mostly from libraries. The environment can often be noisy and competitive. This job requires primarily cold calling and selling, so you definitely need to know how to sell over the phone—and not get offended when someone hangs up on you.

THE CAREER GENIE

The Career Genie looks into his crystal ball to predict the career fortunes of six eager job seekers. What does the future hold for you? Compare yourself to these brave young souls.

~~~~~~~~~~~~~~~~~~~~~~~~~~~~~~~~~~~~~

Bethany

SNAPSHOT

Bethany, 21, hails from Whitefish, Montana. Her parents didn't allow television in the house (poor girl), so Bethany did a lot of reading to entertain herself—everything from *Moby Dick* to *Sweet Valley High* to *It* to *The Corrections*. But she often found herself spending as much time thinking about how the words looked on the page as about the story. She grew to love books as physical objects—and now that's all she gets as presents for birthdays and Christmas. Don't even think about getting this girl a sweater.

She's a perfectionist who loves nothing more than to find—and fix—mistakes. When her watch broke, she took it apart to figure out what happened. Everything she touches must conform to her high standards—but not in some psychotic way. Bethany just likes things to be right and correct. When she watches a movie, for example, she always notices the parts in which a character's shirt was unbuttoned from one camera angle and buttoned from another. Bethany excelled in high school and won a scholarship to the state university. There she keeps to herself, preferring to have a small group of very loyal friends. She's majoring in linguistics and still keeps her head in books, mostly textbooks. Once she found a typo in her Bio 101 book and wrote to alert the publisher to the error. During her first year of college, she joined the staff of the school newspaper; now, as a senior about to graduate, she occasionally writes articles but mostly works on layout and design.

OUTLOOK

Bethany would fit right in at the production department of a university press or at a scholarly, professional, or educational house. Her attention to detail coupled with her background in linguistics would make her a great production editor; that she's extremely well read and knows layout and design would be icing on an already sweet cake. Production work requires a commitment to excellence in style, typography, and grammar, which Bethany definitely has. Life at a scholarly or university press would let Bethany exercise her intellect too: She could learn about new subjects as she checked changes, proofed blues, transferred corrections, and approved the work of her freelancers.

Bethany could better her chances, though, by taking a copyediting or proofreading class. She might also consider taking a publishing course so she could start networking and making some connections in the industry. She may want to come out of her shell a little more, because she'll still have to work with all kinds of people in many different departments. She could join a club or volunteer on campus. Doing a few more extracurricular activities has the added advantage of showing employers that Bethany knows how to manage her time, a key skill for production people. Finally, New York City will be a big change for someone hailing from rural Montana. Nevertheless, it's worth a shot to head there if she wants to work for a big-name house. But since there are plenty of university presses around the country, if she's good, she won't have a problem finding a job anywhere she wants.

Mario

SNAPSHOT

Mario, 21, is from a suburb of Washington, D.C., in northern Virginia. He went to public school, did well, and got into Georgetown University. Even though he technically didn't grow up in D.C., he likes to say that he's from there, and he really does know the city well, having spent tons of time hanging around the hip U Street area. But he's grown kind of tired of the nation's capital, and he's ready to head somewhere bigger where he can meet people and be in the center of things, with his degree in business administration in hand. He's currently concentrating in marketing, and last year he won a prize for a class project: an advertising campaign that tied a new perfume to an upcoming movie. He loves synergizing products, letting hype for one thing (like the perfume) spill over into hype for something else (like the movie).

When Mario isn't maintaining his 3.0 GPA, he's hanging out with anyone and everyone at bars or concerts, promoting the latest party at the No Name Club (where he recently celebrated his 21st birthday), watching movies, getting sucked in by reality television shows, surfing gossip blogs, and flipping through *InTouch* and *People*. He always seems to know who's dating whom (not just celebrities, but around campus too), and people like to pick his brain for advice on what books to read, CDs to buy, and places to shop. It was Mario who started the Georgetown trend of students wearing backpacks on their chests rather than on their backs.

OUTLOOK

Mario's made for the marketing department at a major commercial publishing house. He seems to have his finger on the pulse of pop culture, which is important when trying to figure out the best way to promote books. He also has no fears when it comes to networking and socializing, a must in marketing and publicity. Now that book publishing has expanded into product tie-ins, movies, television shows, and multimedia platforms, houses need marketing specialists and publicists who know how to link people to product and product to product. It doesn't matter whether a house publishes a great book if nobody reads it, and that's where the marketing/publicity department comes in.

Mario will likely impress interviewers with his outgoing personality, but he'll have to work hard to show them that he has the maturity and desire to work in a corporate environment. It would help Mario to do an internship at an office, and it might help too to put his marketing skills to good use by promoting a charity or fundraiser rather than just parties at clubs. Clearly Mario will relish the fast-paced life of New York City, where you often have to make an effort to see the same people twice. But he'll also have to develop patience: It can be tough for some big fishes from the college pond to move to a place like New York, which is a much bigger pond with much bigger fish. He'll have to pay some dues, but with time and devotion, he'll make the contacts and earn the respect of publishing bigwigs, just like he did with campus hot shots in D.C.

Grace

SNAPSHOT

Grace, 25, takes after her name in more ways than one. She's a professional ballet dancer, for one thing, and she's also a Pisces, so she always seems to handle every situation with poise and sensitivity. She's a middle child too, which means she's a pro at accommodating everyone else's needs. Her friends love her good listening skills and respect her thoughtful advice. Somehow she has the answers every time or at least knows whom to ask for the answers. And she has a way of interpreting things (often using elaborate metaphors) that makes people feel better after speaking with her.

Grace doesn't like to think about things in terms of money—she prefers to concentrate on the artistic side of life. Sure, she pays her rent and bills on time every month, and she's been living on her own since she moved to New York at age 16 to attend ballet school. But she'd rather discuss grande pliés than spreadsheets. She collects vintage Broadway playbills, and she's decorated her apartment with ribbons from her various ballet costumes over the years. Her friends were so taken with the scrapbook she made for herself that they asked her to make scrapbooks for them too. Right now she's taking some continuing education classes at Pace University, including English, art history, and biology; she might decide to enroll full-time once she retires from ballet in the next few years.

OUTLOOK

Although nothing about Grace's background links her to publishing, she'd nevertheless find a happy home in design. Her artistic temperament means she'd be a natural at interpreting an author's message into an interior or cover design, and she's already enrolled in an art history course, so she's learning what's been considered "good" and "beautiful" in the past. Also, her experience with scrapbooks shows her creative potential, including an ability to present information visually. She could see if she has the talent and desire for design by taking a hands-on class in Photoshop or InDesign. Grace is also taking an English class, which means she likes books and literature. Whether that translates into an interest in editorial remains to be seen. She could figure out if publishing is for her by working on Pace's literary magazine or by creating her own webzine devoted to ballet or some other interest.

Grace's easygoing, aim-to-please nature would be a great fit at a small, independent press, where she could pitch in and help out in lots of departments. Her ability to talk about an art form—dance—would intrigue employers at a house that specialized in art or coffee table–type books (like Taschen Books, which emphasizes design, look, and feel). To increase her chances of working in publishing, she should definitely earn a BA or BS at Pace. She might also consider doing an internship or two at a publishing house in New York, earning a master's in publishing through Pace, or taking a local publishing course at NYU or Columbia. If she wants to do book design, she'll need to not only master several computer programs but also to develop a portfolio of sample designs.

Erich

SNAPSHOT

Erich, 26, majored in architecture at the Massachusetts Institute of Technology. Originally from Germany, Erich moved with his diplomat mother from

Berlin to Paris to Moscow as a child, then went to high school in the States. He loves to travel and spent a semester abroad in Australia as a junior. No matter where he was, he always kept *The Death and Life of Great American Cities* (Jane Jacobs) and *The Ten Books on Architecture* (Vitruvius) by his side, along with his trusty Nikon.

After completing his degree at MIT, though, Erich decided that as a profession, architecture relies too much on science and math for his tastes. So, along with a few friends, he started a web design firm in Cambridge, Massachusetts. He took a bunch of classes in web developing, programming, and design at Emerson College. While his friends handled the business end, drumming up contacts and drawing up contracts, he handled the creative parts. His portfolio includes sites he designed for a model friend, a record company specializing in emo, an insurance company, a local hospital, and a wedding planner. Now he's decided to focus full-time on graphic design and thinks he might want to get involved in the book business, especially for design-heavy houses like DK and Phaidon. In his spare time, he paints, draws comics, makes his own ice cream, blogs about Beantown architecture, and waits tables at a local wine bar.

OUTLOOK

Erich would totally fit in at the design or web department at a major commercial publishing house. He has the indie cred to know what looks hot to young people and prospective book buyers, plus he has the art savvy that comes with an international background and great education—and he's even done some research to figure out which houses (DK, Phaidon) might be right for him. His website samples show an array of talents, interests, and audiences: The insurance company says, "I know—and respect—corporate life," while the site for his supermodel-to-be pal says, "I'm hip," and the ice cream hobby says, "I don't take myself too seriously." Nonetheless, he's mature enough to convince employers that he has the dedication and passion for a new career.

But if Erich's really, truly serious about a career in publishing, he has to start making connections to the publishing world, and he has to develop a portfolio of interior and jacket designs. He could ask the insurance company if it needs someone to design an office manual, say, or he could head back to Emerson for some classes on typography, illustration, and book design. His résumé should clearly list his ability to use such programs as InDesign, Page-Maker, QuarkXPress, Photoshop, and Illustrator. Finally, he should make sure that his blog is snark-free, because he doesn't want to come off as elitist to prospective employers.

Malia

SNAPSHOT

Malia, 20, is a native New Yorker—born and raised in the fine borough of Brooklyn. After graduating from the prestigious Dalton School, where she was captain of the debate team, she headed to Fordham University to do a double major in English and economics. But part-way through she got burned out and decided to take a year off to try to sell handmade jewelry. She placed a few pieces on consignment in some NoLita boutiques, but she also had to move back in with the 'rents and take a job at Barnes & Noble to support herself. No worries, though, because she loves books. Recently she's decided to use her connections with the trendy boutiques to sell headbands made by her friend Carin, and she's hoping that Carin will give her a cut of any profits.

As soon as she left Fordham, Malia bartered with her friend Chamous: He'd make her some business cards, complete with her cell and email, and she'd make him some bracelets. She now carries these cards everywhere, handing them out to anyone she meets, including a representative from Akashic Books she chatted up at the Brooklyn Literary Festival last week. Now she's got Chamous creating a website for her: www.maliasells.com. Part of her thinks that academic degrees are overrated, but another part of her knows that she needs a BA or BS to succeed—and all of her realizes that at some point, she'll have to get serious about her future. She can't live in her parents' brownstone for the rest of her life.

OUTLOOK

Malia's definitely on her way to a career in sales, and she'd be a great fit for the sales department at any house. Her smooth-talking negotiation skills would help her chances of getting an assistant position, as would her experience selling jewelry, acting as an agent for her friend, and working in retail at Barnes & Noble. The double major in English and economics isn't too shabby either. Finally, her love of reading and arguing would make Malia a natural as a sales rep. And the fact that she's already heading to literary festivals around the city to network is another great big plus.

Just about every publishing house wants its employees to have bachelor's degrees, so Malia will have to head back to school and graduate at some point. But she could go part-time, thereby keeping her schedule open and making sure she's really into publishing before she commits to an entry-level job there. At school, she should take a few business courses in addition to English and economics. Doing some temp work or getting a part-time job in an office would also make her a more desirable candidate, because she'd be showing employers that she knows how to navigate an office environment and handle administrative tasks. Although corporate gigs sometimes have long hours, she'd still be able to make her own jewelry at night and on weekends.

Aki

SNAPSHOT

As a kid in San Francisco, Aki, now 23, loved to stay after class and help his kindergarten teacher erase the chalkboards. During grade school, he asked for extra books and dreaded the long summers, although he liked keeping journals as part of his school's summer reading. As a teen, he joined Quiz Bowl, his school's trivia team (his specialties were science and art), and traveled around the Bay Area. He did well in high school, relishing any chance to give presentations, and he starred in a local production of *Guys and Dolls*. At the University of Dayton, he decided to major in education but realized that, truthfully, he didn't like kids enough to spend the rest of his life working with them. Nevertheless, he decided to fulfill the requirements of the early childhood education major, while adding minors in English and philosophy.

After graduating last year, Aki got a job reviewing books and restaurants for a local alternative newspaper in Dayton, while also posting a popular list of fun things to do in the area on his homepage (called Aki's World). He loves working for a newspaper, but lately he's been craving something else, and his itchy feet want to either head back home to the West Coast or start something new on the East Coast. Aki speaks fluent Japanese, Russian, Spanish, and Hebrew, and, as a sophomore, he lobbied UD to create a dorm for people who want to practice their language skills (no English is allowed, according to Aki's rules); last year, the dorm proved so popular that the school had to create a waiting list.

OUTLOOK

Aki would be a great candidate to work in editorial, particularly for an el-hi or children's book publisher. His major and minors show a diverse range of academic interests; his activities also show diversity, as well as perseverance and a knack for coming up with hit ideas. Publishers love candidates with a proven track record of understanding and conquering a market, as Aki did with his dorm idea and continues to do with his website. The education major, in particular, will give him insight into creating, developing, and updating textbooks and other classroom materials. He'll be able to help educate kids without actually having to deal with them on a daily basis. Aki's writing experience also helps a lot: Someone who knows how to write obviously has the facility with words that editors need in order to be successful.

Aki could up his chances for employment in this competitive field by signing up for a publishing program. Although these programs can be expensive, the opportunity to learn some publishing-specific skills like line editing and proposal writing, as well as the chance to get some face time with industry insiders, would prove invaluable to Aki, who doesn't have too much editorial experience or connections. He could also apply for a yearlong associate's program, which would give him a taste of both publishing and New York for a while. To become even more desirable as an entry-level job seeker, Aki might also take some courses in copyediting and design.

PART II: HOW TO BREAK IN

3

PREPARING YOURSELF FOR THE JOB SEARCH

The deadlines never end, the rules are always changing, the pay is often low, and the hours are very long. So who wants to work in publishing? People who really, really love books. The ones who make it in this business spend their whole professional careers feeling like a kid in a candy store. They're the ones with dedication and passion—they eat, sleep, and breathe their jobs. But you also need certain skills in order to score that dream entry-level job that will put you on the road to a long, lively career in publishing. And that's what this chapter is all about: figuring out what skills you already have, what skills you need to be successful in the various departments, and, finally, how to put those skills onto your résumé.

IDENTIFY KEY SKILLS

We've said it before, and we'll say it again: Publishing works on the apprenticeship model. You start at the bottom, then work your way up as you learn new skills. But it doesn't hurt to work on those skills now. As you read, think about where you fit in. What know-how do you already have? Bear in mind how you'll highlight your knowledge on your résumé. What talents do you need to develop? Consider how you'll develop them as an intern or a volunteer.

66 What skill do I wish I'd had before I started out? Speed reading."

—**Sarah Dickman,** Director of Foreign Rights, Agent
The Nicholas Ellison Agency

Creative Skills

We know "creative skills" is kind of a weird, amorphous way of putting it, but we think this is the best way to describe the innovative, imaginative expertise required of everybody in publishing. After all, the whole point of this industry is to turn ideas into books. Each and every person involved in the process shapes and impacts the final product, so be prepared to show that you have the following skills up your sleeve.

- **Facility with words:** This skill's a big one in publishing, naturally. Salespeople don't just go to their buyers and say, *"Lifeguard. A new book. Buy it."* They use words to describe books to potential buyers. They say, "The latest novel by James Patterson and Andrew Gross tells the action-packed story of Ned Kelley—and an art heist gone very, very wrong." Likewise, design people re-interpret an author's words into a visual format; marketing/publicity people write catalog copy, collate publicity packets, and send out huge mailings; and, of course, editors and production people ensure that all words mean what they're supposed to mean, make sense, and form a coherent, saleable product.

66 My biggest challenge in training editorial assistants is getting them to unlearn everything their English lit professors taught them. The most successful books are written in clear, concise, and plain prose. Think about it: Would you want to read your English thesis on James Joyce and the postcolonial sublime?"

—**Laurie Barnett,** Editor in Chief
SparkNotes

As a publishing professional, you'll be a guardian of the language, even if you specialize in selling graphic novels, so make sure you know the difference between a colon and a semicolon. But you need to know more than just the rules of grammar: You need to write and speak with style and flair. You need to know what makes for a compelling read. The best way to brush up on your word skills is to read. So pick up that copy of a classic you haven't read since high school or subscribe to a magazine that's known for its quality writing (like the *New Yorker*). Reading good stuff will increase your facility with words. A quick review of a grammar handbook will polish your grammar skills, or you could take a copyediting or proofreading class for a more hands-on approach. Whatever you do, always check and recheck all written correspondence (including emails!) for typos.

- **A design sense:** Just as everybody in publishing must develop ideas, so too must everyone in publishing have some sense of what works and doesn't work visually. The best book designs quickly communicate the theme or message of a book. A great cover causes a customer to stop, pick up a book, carry it to a cashier, and, ultimately, take it home. Similarly, a smartly designed packet of publicity materials causes a bookstore owner or librarian to order the book. Good designs spur sales.

  Book designers, in particular, need a finely developed aesthetic, which then gets applied to their choices of color, typography, graphical elements, and illustrations for a particular book. If you're a designer, you should develop a portfolio of sample book designs, including both covers and interiors. The best way to get familiar with things such as typography and graphic design is to take some courses. You'll not only learn the ins and outs, but you'll also get the chance to do some of your own work. Also consider working for your school's literary review or yearbook staff. Editors, managing editors, and publicists should also have the ability to say "yay" or "nay" to the look of a book jacket or interior. A poorly designed book will turn everybody off, and some books, such as "how-tos," have designs that are as important as their content. No matter what, head to a bookstore or library and look through the books there. Take notes about which designs you like and why.

A designer you should know

Chip Kidd has done covers for more than 1,500 books, including *Jurassic Park, Naked, The Secret History,* and *The Wind-Up Bird Chronicle.* He's probably the best-known book designer working today (he's an associate art director at Alfred A. Knopf). In an October 2005 interview with the *New York Post,* Kidd quipped, "Bad covers are usually a product of stupidity, deplorable taste, and editorial cluelessness—and marketing meetings."

- **An ability to recognize good ideas:** Anybody can come up with a great idea for a book—from an agent to an editor to a book packager to a journalist who wrote a few columns about his bad dog (which turned into the super-successful *Marley & Me*) to an everyday young woman stuck on a train (which is exactly how J. K. Rowling dreamed up Harry Potter). But once the idea arrives at a publishing house, it gets polished by lots of people. Every book, from the children's version of *Eats, Shoots & Leaves* to the widely popular *Running with Scissors,* has a team of editors, designers, production managers, publicists, and salespeople behind it. This team decides what the book should look like, as well as where and how it should be sold (and to whom). Everybody on the team pitches in, brainstorms, and contributes.

  An ideal publishing candidate knows a good idea when he sees one, can generate a better idea when another doesn't work, and has the ability to transform a so-so idea into a so-hot idea. He also knows how to articulate and present his idea to others in a captivating and interesting way. Finally, he has to know whether the idea is right for his house: It won't do any good for an editorial assistant at a university press to develop a line of cookbooks, for instance, or to accept a comic book proposal from an agent.

  There's a fine line, too, between recognizing a good idea and recognizing a *profitable* idea. Hundreds of thousands of books get published each year, which means that many, many ideas have been done already—and still more have been rejected along the way. Develop the ability now to think outside the proverbial box by hanging out in bookstores (to see what's getting published); by checking the bestseller lists (to see what's generating sales); by reading or subscribing to publications such as *Publishers Weekly, Kirkus Reviews,* and the *New York Times* (to see what's getting praised and what's getting panned); and by paying attention to trends (to see what's cutting edge). While you're at it, work on developing a thick skin: When you put an idea out there, you risk getting criticized. Learn not to take it personally.

People Skills

Sure, publishing has its share of introverts and people who'd rather groom their pet cats than carry on a conversation. And that works for some people (meow!). But for everybody else, publishing's a social industry with a lot of interaction. Whether you're an editor dealing with authors and agents, a publicist working with journalists and reviewers, a sales rep working with buyers, or a designer working with production editors, you'll always be interacting and collaborating with fellow humans. And you need these skills—and a smile—to do it right.

66 Develop diplomacy! Seriously, many assistants, myself included, come from top universities and are cultured and conditioned to believe that they are destined for greatness. It doesn't matter how high your GPA was or which company your dad is president of: You start at the bottom, as an assistant. A degree of humility and a respect for a system in which persistence and patience is handsomely rewarded with recognition and promotion would have served me well."

—**Arija Weddle,** Agent's Assistant/Agent-in-Training
The Nicholas Ellison Agency

- **A talent for playing nicely with others:** It's true that *teamwork* is one of those jargony words commonly found in human resources materials. Nevertheless, getting along with others is an underrated— and extremely valuable—skill. You'll be working with all kinds of people (and their egos) to facilitate the creation of a book. Teamwork involves respecting everyone's opinion, as well as knowing and sticking to your role in the process.

    Most important, you need to know when to speak up and when not to; after all, no matter how strongly you feel about something, you are one of many. When you feel you must, contribute your opinion, but don't push when it's clear that everybody else has moved on or disagrees. For example, if you're a production editor, refrain from being too critical of a book's design unless you think the font's too small for people to comfortably read the book. If you're in design, don't make negative comments about an author's writing unless you're absolutely sure that it's trash. Know your place. As they say, there's no *i* in *team,* and people who don't get along with others will quickly find themselves not getting along with others in unemployment lines.

- **Communication skills:** "Can you hear me now?" isn't just a tagline for a cell phone company; it's also an example of a must-have workplace skill: the ability to communicate. To be a good communicator, you need not only to be articulate in your speech and writing but to also be a good listener. As an editor, you're essentially a representative of the publishing house. You'll constantly be talking with people—new authors, veteran authors, and literary agents about new ideas or books; publicists and salespeople about how to sell the book and develop a platform for the author; and even magazines and newspapers to create a buzz about hot new titles. You're the author's number-one advocate within the publishing house, so you'll always be communicating to bigwigs on her behalf.

  As a salesperson, you'll need to be able to rattle off titles appropriate to whomever you're talking to at the moment. If you're on the phone with book buyers in Minnesota, you might not want to pitch them *The Girls' Guide to Manhattan,* but you'll definitely want to pique their interest about your house's other titles, including *Everything You Wanted to Know About Fly-Fishing but Were Afraid to Ask.* As a publicist, you can't create a buzz if you don't like talking to people or running book events. Plus, you need to be passionate and eloquent in order to generate excitement about the books. If you don't care, nobody else will either.

  If you're still in school, work on your communication skills by taking classes that force you to write, participate in discussions, and give presentations. If you're out of college, you can still perfect your ability to speak and listen well by . . . (drumroll, please) going to parties. We're not advocating that you head to all-out bacchanalias; rather, you should head to industry lectures, panel discussions, literary readings, gallery openings, and any other event that will force you to have conversations with people you don't know. Socializing lets you work on your communication skills while networking—a winning combination.

66 One of the hardest parts of publicity is calling reporters/journalists in the middle of the day to talk to them about the book you're working on. More often than not, they're working on a deadline and don't want to be interrupted—which leads to some very crisp/curt responses if they do pick up the phone. I wasn't ready for that when I first started out. And sometimes it still feels like a cold breeze through the phone."

—**Colleen Schwartz,** Senior Publicist
St. Martin's Press

- **An aptitude for smooth talking:** We don't mean you have to sound like Barry White, but you do need to know how to negotiate and persuade, particularly if you plan to dominate in editorial, marketing/ publicity, or sales. But smooth talking's different from being able to communicate: Communication skills allow you to dole out and process information, whereas smooth talking means you can induce someone to do what you want. It sounds creepy, but it's not. An editor must be able to convince an agent that she understands the vision of the book, then negotiate to secure the best royalty rates for her house. She must also persuade the publisher to "buy" the manuscript. After she's acquired the manuscript, the editor must persuade the rest of the publishing team, especially sales reps, that the book will sell. Publicists persuade the media that the book is worth the public's attention, and they must negotiate for author interviews, book reviews, and advertising space. A good salesperson obviously has stellar negotiation and persuasion skills.

  To some degree, smooth talking comes with time and experience. A great way to develop your negotiation and persuasion skills, though, is to work in retail. Experience selling any product, whether books or toothpaste, will help to hone these skills.

Organizational and Strategic-Thinking Skills

Staying organized means the difference between spending your time doing your work and spending your time looking for the work you need to do. A neat desk, clearly labeled folders full of papers, an up-to-date calendar, a systematic way of processing royalty statements or other documents,

Events such as book signings, author readings, author interviews, and book parties help drive sales. If you have experience organizing people, mention it on your résumé.

and an office notebook that you carry with you everywhere are hallmarks of the organized employee. Regardless of which department you work in, publishing demands that you handle multiple projects in many different stages. Creative or people skills mean nothing if you're unable to use these skills in an organized and strategic way. Read on to see what we mean.

- **Project-management experience:** Publishing's a manufacturing business, so getting the books made is everybody's top priority. Knowing your role in the process is key. In order to make sure the projects get done on time and done right, you'll have to be aware of how a bunch of different elements get turned into a book. Although the production/manufacturing team generally oversees the entire production process, every department needs to effectively manage its parts, whether it's overseeing the author's writing schedule, planning an author event, reviewing page proofs, making a sale to a buyer, getting the covers designed in time for a marketing push, mailing ARCs to a reviewer, signing off on covers with the manufacturer, or sending the files off to the printer. One missed deadline has the potential to derail the entire schedule. No joke.

    Project management involves knowing the schedule a book is on, who's doing what, which elements are missing, and when those elements will be completed. It involves making sure your projects—and people—are on track. It's helpful to keep an eye on projects using a database program such as Excel. Production people in particular use Excel to develop complex schedules that track books as they move through the copyediting, proofing, indexing, reviewing, typesetting, and shipping stages.

- **Time-management skills:** Being able to manage your projects effectively goes hand in hand with being able to mange your time effectively. We all get the same amount of minutes in a day; the difference stems from how we use those minutes. Books run on tight schedules. Like project management, time management involves setting priorities: Do you need to first file the royalty statements or comb through the slush pile? You'll also need to develop the ability to quickly assess how much time your projects might require. In publishing, deadlines are absolutes.

Sometimes publishers **crash**, or rush, a book to capitalize on a trend or an event. Whereas a typical book might have a one- or two-year-long writing, editing, and production schedule, a crashed title might go from idea to bound book in a couple of months.

The production/manufacturing department maintains master schedules of all the projects being published over a period of years. They quickly learn which editors and designers hand their work in on time—and which don't—and they dole out treatment accordingly. Production and design also assigns its freelancers due dates, as do editors with their authors, so you can't be afraid to create deadlines and stick to them. As a sales rep, you'll need to set your own hours and figure out how to get from one bookstore to the next, with your game face on, ready to sell some books. Procrastinating might have been fun (or funny) in college, but in the working world, time really is money.

You can do it!

At the risk of sounding self-helpy, everybody has project- and time-management skills After all, life in the twenty-first century keeps getting more complicated, as we program our cell phones to check our email and watch TV on our iPods. But you can further develop your multitasking mastery by planning and executing a project of your own, such as a constantly updated blog devoted to a favorite topic (keep it positive, not snarky), coaching a kids' athletic team, or teaching a class at a local community center. Likewise, don't just study all the time or work all the time. Show your ability to manage your minutes by getting a part-time job if you're still in college or volunteering or taking continuing education classes if you've already entered the workforce. What you do isn't nearly as important as demonstrating your ability to do more than one thing at a time and to see all those things through to completion.

- **Market savvy:** Knowing trends and the target audience for your house's projects will make generating and shaping ideas much easier. You need to be strategic, always figuring out how to build a better mousetrap—er, book. You can't get people excited about a book if you aren't familiar with the very people you're trying to sell to. You'll need to know what those people are reading, watching, wearing, discussing, buying, eating, drinking, gossiping about, and listening to.

66 Think like your target customers. Know what motivates them to take your product to the register."

—**Greg Oviatt,** Senior Editor
Barnes & Noble

In addition to knowing what's hot, you need to be aware of what your competitors are doing. Every house vies with every other for sales, so how can you help your house sell more books? It's up to you to figure out why some books go into 10 printings within the first month. Analyzing the difference between a book bound for bestsellerdom and a book bound for the remainder table isn't easy, but it helps to know which books seem to captivate your target market and to theorize about why.

Designers should know the latest in color and font. Some covers have timeless appeal, and others might piggyback on the success of one season's hit. For example, the popularity of *The Da Vinci Code* led to an increased use of gold and red on covers. Yup, it's true.

Surfin' savvy

Our media-saturated culture makes it much easier to identify trends. Every predilection under the sun has its own magazine, website, or blog. And publishers now pay a great deal of attention to who's saying what on the Internet, especially after the web-driven success of *Home Land,* by Sam Lipsyte. Picador quietly published the novel in late 2004. But several bloggers wrote about how much they loved the book, which led to positive reviews on Amazon and other places on the web, which led to huge turnouts at Lipsyte's readings across the country, which, of course, led to super-high sales.

The website Technorati.com lets you search blogs in real time to find the latest info on a person, trend, book, or idea. It also posts users' favorite blogs, sites, and videos. Other online must-reads for juicy publishing tidbits include Beatrice.com, Bookslut.com, Gawker.com, and MaudNewton.com.

Develop your market savvy by pulling out some key themes from the cultural miasma. Are vampires hot right now? Albinos with secrets (thank you, Dan Brown)? No carbs, some carbs, diets named after regions of the United States? You'll also want to think like your audience. For example, if you want to work in educational publishing for high school students, read such magazines as *Teen Vogue* or *Teen People* to start to think like your readers. If your friends ask why you've developed a sudden interest in *Laguna Beach* or *One Tree Hill*, tell them you're "doing research."

Computer and Technical Skills

Gone are the days of pasting corrections to poster-board mockups, pecking out manuscripts on a typewriter, and fixing errors with liquid paper (aka Wite-Out). Publishing relies on computers to do everything from formatting a manuscript to tracking production costs to calculating specs to running the printer that actually prints the books. But humans need to tell the computers what to do, so make sure you know how to do more than just click around the Internet before applying for a publishing job.

- **Desktop publishing:** Desktop publishing software includes InDesign, QuarkXPress, Adobe Photoshop, Adobe PageMaker, and Adobe Illustrator. These programs are especially important for people in design and production, but editors also need to have an understanding of what can—and cannot—be done by the publishing programs. Everybody needs to know how to use regular word-processing programs, and it would be super-helpful to also know how to use data-management programs such as Excel. If you don't know how to use these programs or if you could use a refresher, take a class at a local community college or center for continuing education.

P&L: Editors prepare "profit-and-loss" reports for all of their projects to estimate price, costs, specs, discounts, and, most important, potential profit.

- **Number crunching:** Think publishing only involves words? Think again, mister. Publishing is a business, and, as such, a lot of numbers are involved. Production and manufacturing must find the right materials and determine costs. Editors and publishers must estimate advances and royalties. A sales rep's salary often directly links to the number of books she's sold. Every department has a budget from which it pays freelancers and deducts other expenses, including everyone's bonus during review time.

- **Copyediting and proofreading symbols:** Less important for people in sales or marketing/publicity, knowledge of the marks used by copy editors, compositors, and proofers is a must-have for editors, designers, and production editors. These little marks tell people what to do to the text: Delete words, transpose letters, start a new paragraph, add a period, and so on. Buy yourself a copy of the *Chicago Manual of Style* and flip through it. Also consider taking a class in copyediting or proofreading. You won't be expected to have this stuff memorized by the time you start an entry-level job, but you should be familiar with the symbols.

Proofreading symbols

A ton of books out there teach copyediting and proofreading, and some, such as *The Copyeditor's Handbook,* even include exercises for practice. To get you started, we've included some common proofreading symbols and their meanings below.

Symbol	Meaning
∧	Insert
⟋	Delete
⁋	Make new paragraph
⋏	Insert a comma
⌒	Delete space; close up
#	Insert space
ⓢⓟ	Spell out
ⓢⓣⓔⓣ	Stet (let it stand; don't change)

CRAFT A KILLER RÉSUMÉ

You could have all the skills in the world, but what you know won't matter a lick if your résumé sucks. That little piece of paper most certainly makes or breaks you as a job candidate. Publishing traffics in words, so one typo and your résumé will get filed—in the circular filing cabinet. Think of your résumé as a calling card. It lets the folks in HR and the department hiring managers know who you are, where you've been, what you know, and what you can do.

Don't dread doing your résumé. Instead, see it as a chance to toot your own horn. Now's not the time to be bashful or modest. Now's also not the time to make careless mistakes or bury your skills beneath reams of prose. So, to make sure your résumé is awesome, follow the 10 tips below.

1. **Figure out what to emphasize.** Your résumé should emphasize three major areas: education, work experience, and skills. Use the top of the page for the things that employers really want in their entry-level employees: administrative skills (office experience), project-management skills, and computer skills. If you went to an impressive school or if you had a kick-ass GPA, stick it prominently (but not obnoxiously) at the top of your résumé; otherwise, list it at the bottom. Having some kind of real publishing experience, such as an internship, goes a long way toward making your résumé stand out from the pack. But don't forget transferable skills. Working at a bookstore, tutoring kids, or even bartending shows that you're a decent person who's not afraid of hard work.

2. **Explain your objective.** Some people just begin their résumé with their education, but if you're coming from a nontraditional background or changing from another industry, consider beginning with an objective statement. An objective statement will clarify what you're applying for (internship or entry-level position) and where specifically you want to work (children's books, managing editorial).

3. **Keep it to one page.** This rule's unbreakable. Nobody has the time to read through pages and pages of everything you've done since junior high—and frankly, having a résumé that's longer than a page when you're just starting out makes you look pompous and self-important.

Use your résumé to spark someone's interest. Save the stories and explanations for the interview.

4. **Make it look nice.** We're not kidding here. Your résumé should be as pretty as can be, because it helps employers form an impression of you. Complicated, ugly résumés with small fonts will aggravate professionals in an industry, such as publishing, where looks (of words) matter. Use a font large enough to decipher without squinting (11 or 12 point), and use a typeface that works well in Word or over email such as Times New Roman or Georgia. Finally, remember to avoid long blocks of text. Use bullets instead. Don't use brightly colored paper or wacky fonts just to draw attention to your résumé. Sure, we've all heard the story of the enthusiastic young job seeker who so wanted to become an editorial assistant that she printed her résumé in such a way that it resembled a book. But that's the office equivalent of an urban legend. In the real world, neatness and elegance always triumph over gimmicks.

5. **Categorize your experience.** There are two ways to organize your experience in a résumé: chronologically or functionally. A chronological résumé lists your education and employment in order, with the most recent experience at the top of the page. (The sample résumés of Andrew Feather and Virgil Gotti later in this chapter are organized chronologically.) A functional résumé groups your employment by category. (Melinda Levy's sample résumé on page 104 is organized functionally.) For example, you might divide your work experience into three large categories that clearly relate to jobs in publishing: writing (for your school's literary magazine), administrative experience (working in the admissions office part time), and educational experience (volunteering at a book club for inner-city teens). By creating these categories on your résumé, you've shown that you have three very specialized skills. And if your experience matches the experiences we've listed, bravo. Now consider applying for an editorial assistant position at an educational publisher.

6. **Make it snappy.** Action verbs rule! They make your activities sound specific, impressive, and involved. Give your action verbs as much action as possible: Instead of *did,* try *managed;* instead of *helped,* try *supported;* instead of *read,* try *analyzed* or *edited.* Other good words for

publishing: *communicated, drafted, organized,* and *solved.* Your résumé should read like an exciting advertisement of the professional you. It should list all the things you've done thus far in the most attention-grabbing way. Go out of your way to plug yourself, but never, ever cross the line into misrepresenting or lying about your actual experience.

7. **But keep it professional.** No pictures, no date of birth, and no inappropriate email addresses such as "nkstuddlypimp@geemail.com" should come within spitting distance of your résumé. Likewise for any info about high school, even if you were president of the student body and champion pole-vaulter. Your résumé serves as your introduction to potential employers. They'll be checking it out to see not only whether you can do the job but also to make sure that you'll be a good fit personality-wise.

66 When I interviewed for my first publishing job at Scientific American, my double biology-English degree interested the editors, as did a prize I won in college for an English paper. It turned out that the subject of the paper, Carson McCullers, was one of the copy chief's favorite authors. So the more angles someone looking for that first job can come up with to put on the résumé, the better the chance of connecting with someone."

—**Karen Taschek,** Editor/Writer
Taschek Trade and Tech

8. **Do a real-world check.** Find job listings for positions similar to the ones you're interested in and compare your résumé to the requirements called for in the ad. If you've got most of them covered in your résumé, you'll be a competitive candidate. Otherwise, figure out how you can tweak your experience (without lying!) to fill in the gaps.

9. **Proofread . . . and proofread again.** Imagine your friend comes over to you wearing a beautiful yellow dress. As she gets closer, though, you notice a small blue stain. Soon that stain becomes the only thing you can see. Well, typos are like stains on your résumé. An errant period, a misspelled word, or a misplaced modifier is all it takes for a human

resources person to chuck your résumé, especially in the world of publishing. If you can't represent your best self now, how would you represent the company as an employee? Don't rely on spell-check to catch all your mistakes. Read it carefully, read it again, and then get someone else to read it. Double- and triple-check any names against the job ad or website.

❝ I've seen résumés thrown out for misspelling the name of the company (*and*, not *&*) on a cover letter. Use spell-check and have a friend with a good eye look over your résumé and cover letter."

—Anne Heausler, Editor
Holt, Rinehart and Winston

10. **Get advice.** Make sure you get an outsider's opinion on your résumé once you've finished it. While a person with publishing experience would be an ideal reader, anyone with some business experience will work. The friendly faces at your college career center are also valuable resources. Don't just thrust the résumé into someone's open hands; instead, ask your reader for specific feedback. Say something like, "Do you think the chronological style works?" Any pair of fresh eyes will be able to scan the document quickly, letting you know which words or skills stand out. Trade a friend a beer for a quick résumé read. (But buy the beer after he reads it.)

SAMPLE RÉSUMÉS

Now that you've mastered these tips, we'll show you the résumés of three job-seekers looking for entry-level jobs. Each applicant comes to the table with different backgrounds, but they all follow the 10 steps to a T, creating clear, well-designed résumés that market themselves as compellingly as possible. Read their résumés and our commentaries, then get inspired to write your own!

SAMPLE RÉSUMÉ—DESIGN ASSISTANT

Melinda M. Levy

54321 Hickory Lane, Greenwich, CT 12345   123-444-8868   melindamlevy@yahee.com

Objective: To obtain an entry-level position in the design department of a commercial publishing house.

Education
University of Virginia, Charlottesville, VA
Bachelor of Arts, English, 2007

Skills
Computer: Excel, Access, Outlook, QuarkXPress, InDesign, Photoshop, PageMaker
Languages: Spanish   **Other:** Writing, Singing, Dancing, Teaching

Publishing Experience
La UVA Monthly **magazine,** Charlottesville, VA
Writer and Layout Editor   2005–2007
- Wrote twenty-four articles for the "Nightlife" section, including:
    "Can Delta Delta Help Ya?: UVA's Social Fund-raisers," "Playing the Field: The Dating Woes of College
    Athletes," "Bored Without Board Games: The Nightlife of the Night-In Subculture," and "Above Par Bar:
    The Best Bars"
- Developed a new template and masthead design
- Designed the layout for every issue, including placement of photographs, illustrations,
  and advertisements

Administrative Experience
UVA Undergraduate Admissions Office, Charlottesville, VA
Administrative Assistant   2004–2006
- Maintained database of all undergraduate applications
- Answered phone and email inquiries regarding undergraduate admissions
- Scheduled on-campus interviews for admissions committee
- Compiled and mailed admissions packets for all accepted students

Teaching Experience
Edith B. Jackson Day Care Center, New Haven, CT
Assistant Caregiver   2004
- Assisted in providing day care to children ranging from one to four years of age
- Led activities that aid in childhood development and taught preschoolers how to read and write

Signing with Kids, Fairfax, VA
Intern/Teacher, "Mommy and Me" Classes   2003
- Taught eight-week sign language class to parents and their children in order to promote earlier child-
  parent communication

Restaurant Experience
P.F. Chang's China Bistro, McLean, VA
Server   2002

Design portfolio available upon request.

What's So Great About Melinda's Résumé?

1. **She states her objective.** Employers prefer employees who know what they want when it comes to jobs, rather than someone who'll take whatever job she can get. Begin your résumé by expressing exactly what type of job you want (and make sure that job fits the want ad description). Follow that up with clear evidence of your qualifications, and you'll get noticed.

2. **She makes the organization work.** Melinda organizes her résumé to highlight her strengths. She puts her education at the top, since she graduated from a well-known school. Then she clearly groups her skills so employers can see that she already knows how to use a range of publishing programs. Companies like someone who already knows how to do things: Less time spent training someone translates to higher worker productivity and more $$$. Brutal, but true.

3. **She categorizes her experience.** Melinda's had just a wee bit of experience in publishing (working on her college magazine), but she highlights the fact that she *has* publishing experience by creating experience categories. Melinda smartly puts "publishing experience" first, then follows it with "administrative experience," since that's crucial for any entry-level job. Even though her other experience categories aren't directly related to publishing, she puts them on her résumé to show that she's a hard worker with people skills.

4. **She gives details.** Melinda doesn't just give dates, locations, and positions; she gives details—the all-important, in-depth descriptions of what she did. Rather than say simply "writer and designer," Melinda lists how many articles she wrote, where those articles appeared, and even gives a few titles. Likewise, she specifically explains what she did at the "Mommy and Me" classes. By giving the time frame, she demonstrates her ability to successfully manage a project to completion.

5. **She uses consistent formatting of all elements.** Notice that all of the names of companies are in bold and the names of positions are in italic. Très eye catching. This seems like a minor point, but don't discount aesthetics when it comes to your résumé. Always strive for elegance and attractiveness. Remember: Your résumé is the first impression an employer has of you—just like you wouldn't wear sneakers and a track suit to a job interview, don't use funky fonts and wacky words on your résumé.

6. **She says she has a portfolio available upon request.** She realizes that the position for which she's applying—"design assistant"—requires samples, so she tells employers that she's got them ready.

SAMPLE RÉSUMÉ—EDITORIAL ASSISTANT
Andrew Feather

12345 Melrose Drive | 718-555-1234
Brooklyn, NY 54321 | afeather@myemail.com

Experience
Random House Associates Program (Intern)
New York, NY   *July–August 2006*

- Rotated through the editorial, production, marketing, publicity, and sales departments of the Knopf imprint
  - » *Editorial:* answered phones; trafficked manuscripts to production for copyediting; transmitted manuscripts, proofs, and publicity materials to authors for review; read slush pile searching for publishable material
  - » *Production:* prepared pages for other departments for review; updated production schedules; faxed corrections to typesetter
  - » *Marketing:* maintained database for mailings; mailed marketing materials
  - » *Publicity:* assisted in preparing press kits; coordinated mailing of press kits to publications, radio stations, television shows, and bookstores
  - » *Sales:* packaged sales catalogs for sales representatives

The Lantern (Reporter)
Columbus, OH   *October 2003–June 2006*

- Reported on political issues important to students on campus, including race, class, ethnicity, abortion, immigration, human rights, free speech, religious persecution, international trade
- Hosted roundtable discussions on the above topics and transcribed the discussions for publication in *The Lantern*

New York City Public School System (Substitute Teacher)
New York, NY   *September 2006–present*

- Prepare and facilitate lesson plans in math, English, computer skills, biology, technology, music, and Spanish
- Teach various age groups and academic levels in intensive group settings and larger classes of 30 to 40 students

Education
The Ohio State University, Columbus, OH
Bachelor of Arts, English (cum laude), June 2006

Awards
National Buckeye Scholar (annual merit scholarship)
Robert E. Reiter Prize for Critical Analysis, Department of English, The Ohio State University

Skills
Internet Explorer, Excel, Access, Outlook

References available upon request.

What's So Great About Andrew's Résumé?

1. **He highlights his strengths.** Andrew has awesome publishing experience, so he rightly puts that at the top. His education's not too shabby either, but the Random House program definitely trumps OSU (sorry, Buckeyes). He goes even further by listing out the various departments he worked in at Knopf. Always put your best stuff—whether experience, education, GPA, awards, or skills—at the top of your résumé.

2. **He uses active language.** All told, Andrew includes 17 action verbs in his résumé. Notice too how he uses different verbs for the same skills—that is, rather than simply say *mailed* over and over again, he says that he *coordinated mailings, packaged,* and *transmitted.* Same skill set, sure, but the different words make the skill sound more robust. Use active words in your résumé and go for variety.

3. **He speaks the language of publishing.** Andrew gives extremely specific information about his experience at Random House by using publishing vocabulary. Words and phrases such as *trafficked manuscripts, transmitted proofs, slush pile,* and *press kits* let employers know that he's serious about a career in publishing. These words also show that Andrew already has some skills, which means employers can spend less time training him in the basics and more time giving him real work to do—a major advantage.

4. **He lists his accomplishments.** Andrew points out that he earned a merit scholarship and won a prize for an English paper. If you won an award—any award—in college, put it on your résumé.

5. **He uses bullet points for clarity.** Bullet points not only look nice and neat, they also make it easy for readers to find key information. Andrew made it very simple for employers to see the wide range of stuff he did at Random House by tabbing in, bolding and italicizing the different departments, and explaining the various work he performed after each bullet.

6. **He says he has references available upon request.** Although not every job application requires references, it's always good to note that you have them. Mentioning the possibility of references shows employers that you've impressed other bosses enough that they'd be willing to speak on your behalf.

SAMPLE RÉSUMÉ–MARKETING ASSISTANT

VIRGIL GOTTI

2000 Butch Cassidy Drive, Astoria, NY 10001 • 333-555-7777 • virgil@hotmaile.com

EDUCATION:
Davidson College, Davidson, NC, May 2005
Bachelor of Arts, Philosophy
Bachelor of Science, Math (double major)
Phi Beta Kappa, Cumulative GPA: 3.9

HONORS:
High Honors in Math
Davidson College Scholar Athlete, Fall 2004
Dean's List, 2003–2005

SKILLS:
GENERAL: positive attitude, hardworking, detail oriented, organized, communication skills
LANGUAGE: excellent writing/typing skills, minor proficiency in Italian and Hebrew
COMPUTER: proficient in Microsoft Word, Excel, PowerPoint, Outlook, Explorer, FrontPage, Publisher, Adobe Reader and Adobe Illustrator; proficient in both PC and MAC OS

ACTIVITIES & INTERESTS:
Equestrian Team member, Italian Club historian, WOZQ Radio fund-raising board member, WOZQ deejay, member of United in Anti-Racist Action, SOS Community Service, Literary Fiction

EXPERIENCE:
KNF&T STAFFING AGENCY (New York, NY), *Temporary Worker, June 2005–present*
- Agency's first-call employee for last-minute temporary assignments
- Extensive experience in a variety of work environments, including the following:

DANA FARBER CANCER INSTITUTE, *Clinical Research Coordinator, May 2006–present*
- Update clinical research databases using Microsoft Access, Outlook, and Excel; code patient data and communicate with all departmental representatives
- Lead data acquisition efforts by contacting more than 300 hospitals, doctors' offices, and health-care centers
- Prepare weekly presentations for department meetings using Microsoft Excel and PowerPoint
- Work closely with resident nurses and research doctors to draft and file clinical research forms for all on-trial patients
- Become conversant with all DFCI databases for coding all drug treatment cycles, radiological scans, and lab work
- Track patient appointments and conduct patient screening to determine protocol eligibility

PEARSON EDUCATION, *Front Desk/Administrative Assistant, October 2005–May 2006*
- Served as initial contact for employees and guests of Pearson Education
- Answered phones, filed mail, typed correspondence, and data entry using Microsoft Excel

HOUGHTON MIFFLIN PUBLISHING CO., *Data Entry, July 2005*
- Data entry and database management
- Update changes in various classroom textbook editions using in-house software

LANDVEST REAL ESTATE, *Office Assistant, June 2005*
- Managed mass mailing of new property listings to Landvest Clients
- Answered phones, communicated with brokers about new listings and open house information

What's So Great About Virgil's Résumé?

1. **He focuses on his administrative experience.** Virgil doesn't have very much direct publishing experience, but he has worked in a lot of different office environments. Virgil's résumé proves him to be a man who knows his way around an office—a good thing to be when applying for entry-level jobs, which require a lot of administrative work.

2. **He names databases and software.** By listing specific databases and software, Virgil shows that he's computer literate and adapts quickly to new environments.

3. **He highlights his progress.** In just a few months at Dana Farber, Virgil has moved from tracking patient appointments to handling PowerPoint presentations. Temping's a good way to make a few bucks while earning administrative experience, but temping also gives you an important skill: It lets you show employers how adaptable you are.

4. **He lists skills and interests related to publishing.** Virgil says that he has a "positive attitude," a must for marketing people, who have to bring a heavy dose of enthusiasm to the 9-to-5 grind in order to get others excited about specific books. It might feel hokey to sing your own praises, but your résumé is not the place for modesty. Virgil also notes that he enjoys "literary fiction." Don't just list "reading" on your résumé; employers already know you like books, since you're applying for a job in publishing. Instead, be specific about the types of books you like to read.

5. **He keeps it professional.** Virgil's résumé uses consistent formatting, bold, and small caps for emphasis. He gives specific information, such as the number of hospitals he contacted as part of the "data acquisition efforts." Although he doesn't have publishing experience, he uses words common to publishing, including *communicate, in-house,* and *acquisition.* Finally, Virgil makes it very easy for the employer to see the wide range of skills and experience he has by using headings and bullets for legibility and scannability.

6. **He's honest.** Rather than claim fluency in Italian or Hebrew, Virgil notes that he has "minor proficiency." He also uses indents to make it clear that he worked at Pearson and Houghton Mifflin as a temp. Lying on your résumé is a gigantic no-no.

4

BECOMING AN EXPERT

Here, we'll show you how to learn everything there is to know about publishing before you apply for that entry-level dream job. Now's the time to really explore your passion. This means gathering more information, reading all there is to read, building your network, and getting psyched about yourself and your chosen career field. The more you know, the more excited you'll be about publishing—and the more desirable a candidate you'll become to publishers.

READ, READ, READ

It's no surprise that an industry all about words is the subject of a ton of magazines, books, and websites. You don't have to read every one, of course, but you should be familiar with them all, since these are what your colleagues, hiring managers, and, most important, bosses read in their spare time.

66 Read as many book reviews as you can to see what's coming out and what subjects are popular right now and keep up with the bestseller lists to see what's selling. This info will also be useful in a job interview and shows that you're interested in keeping up."

—**Hilary Terrell,** Assistant Editor
Gotham Books

Trade Magazines

The magazines below will tell you everything you need to know about who's getting promoted (which means a position might be opening up . . .), what's on its way to being a bestseller, and who's publishing what.

- **Publishers Weekly:** This weekly magazine covers publishing industry news, as well as major trends and developments, including who's in, who's out, and who's collecting severance pay. The back half of the magazine is devoted to book reviews, long considered to be "the industry standard." *PW* also maintains a very comprehensive website at publishersweekly.com, with job listings, industry resources, book reviews, bestseller lists, and a pub date calendar (which outlines each season's hottest titles).

- **Publishing Trends:** A monthly newsletter full of news and opinions on trends in the industry. It also lists recent promotions and hirings. Most professionals get the newsletter in the form of a PDF in their email inbox. Go to publishingtrends.com for details.

- **Kirkus Reviews:** This biweekly publication contains reliable reviews written by specialists in relevant fields (so a doctor will review a book about medicine, for example). The magazine reviews 5,000 titles annually in practically every genre under the sun, including mystery, science fiction, and self-help. *Kirkus* also has a free email newsletter; sign up at kirkusreviews.com.

- **Library Journal:** The self-proclaimed "one-stop" source for library professionals and distributors who handle the library market. This magazine is another great source of reviews of books, audiobooks, and DVDs. Check out its website at libraryjournal.com.

- **Horn Book Magazine:** Published bimonthly, *Horn Book Magazine* features book reviews and articles on almost every children's and YA book produced in the United States. These reviews and articles are also published semiannually as *The Horn Book Guide,* which also includes an extensive index. Check out its website at hbook.com.

- **Bookmarks Magazine:** Can't find anything to read? Pick up the one and only publication about books written especially for the avid reader! This magazine rates new books based on evaluations of reviews from all major publications, and it also publishes summaries, reader recommendations, and in-depth author biographies. Check it out at bookmarksmagazine.com.

Recommended Books

Books about publishing books? Don't tell us you're surprised. The books below not only give great information about the industry in general but also discuss such specifics as salaries, types of jobs, publishing jargon, and tips for the job hunt. You'll definitely want to add these puppies to your own personal library.

- *The Book Publishing Industry,* by Albert N. Greco, Lawrence Erlbaum Associates, 2004
  Everyone in the industry should own this book. It's a great resource for learning about the state of publishing today. The charts and tables sometimes make it a little dry, but the high quality of the information more than compensates for the occasional dusty turn of phrase. Greco thoughtfully and objectively covers such topics as distribution channels, business operations, marketing, intellectual property, and mergers and acquisitions.

- *Book Business: Publishing Past, Present, and Future,*
  by Jason Epstein, W.W. Norton, 2002
  Many consider Epstein to be the founder of the trade paperback—and he edited some of the greatest contemporary writers around, including Vladimir Nabokov and Jane Jacobs. Based on a series of lectures Epstein gave at the New York Public Library, this professional memoir chronicles the publishing industry from as early as the nineteenth century and offers his expert predictions on the industry's transformations in the future.

- *The Business of Books,* by Andre Shriffen, Schriffen, verso, 2000
  Formerly the head of Pantheon Books, Schriffen discusses what he considers to be the sad decline of American publishing. He blames the decline on the media conglomerates' steady gobbling up of the independents, and he discusses the effect of the Internet boom

on the industry. A discouraging yet realistic look at the state of the industry.

- ***On Publishing,*** by Lionel Leventhal, Greenhill Books, 2006
  A professional memoir, *On Publishing* recounts the author's life journey in the publishing industry. Founder of Arms & Amour Press, the London Book Fair, and Greenhill Books, Leventhal provides an inside look at British and intercontinental publishing. There's no better way to learn about the industry than reading about the life of an industry giant.

66 The more well read you are, the more you'll enjoy your job. 'Well read' doesn't mean classics either—it means a little bit of everything, from pop culture to children's books to memoirs to political thrillers."

—**Colleen Schwartz,** Senior Publicist
St. Martin's Press

Logging On

Who doesn't love the Internet? It lets you check up on old boyfriends, order shoes, peruse the menu for the hot new bistro down the street, touch base with your parents, check the latest MLB standings, and learn more about publishing—all without leaving your desk.

WEBSITES

- **Publishers Marketplace,** publishersmarketplace.com
  Be sure to sign up for their daily email newsletter, *Publishers Lunch,* for the latest goings-on in the industry, including recent acquisitions and deals. Everybody who's anybody in publishing reads this one.

- **Booklist Online,** booklistonline.com
  Geared toward librarians, *Booklist*'s free website contains a searchable database of more than 100,000 book reviews. Don't forget to subscribe to the newsletter too.

- **BookWeb,** bookweb.org
  The electronic home of the American Booksellers Association (ABA), an organization of independent booksellers. Be sure to check out Book Sense, ABA's program for promoting eclectic books chosen as favorites by independent booksellers. Book Sense distributes a newsletter containing "Book Sense Picks" and also produces a widely distributed nationwide bestseller list.

- **BookWire,** bookwire.com
  Great industry resource with extensive links and information on new books, authors, and industry trends.

- **Bookslut,** bookslut.com
  Don't be creeped out by the name: Written by avid readers and writers, this e-magazine features book reviews, columns, and author interviews. There's not a single piece of porn in sight.

- **WritersDigest.com**
  This website is a must for writers seeking to publish their work. It features a bookstore, online workshops, information about writers' conferences, a book club, an email newsletter, and a link to the *Writer's Market,* a searchable database of editors and agents.

- **Mediabistro.com**
  Probably the hottest site on the web for professionals in all media industries. It features job postings, industry resources, and forums, as well as information about networking events and career development seminars.

- **ArtsJournal,** artsjournal.com/publishing
  Go here for a daily digest with direct links to interesting stories from more than 200 publications covering culture and the arts.
  You can also have the digest sent to you as an email newsletter.

- **TheBookseller.com**
  This site primarily covers the international publishing world,

especially what's happening in the United Kingdom. It publishes daily news and opinion, author interviews, career advice, recruitment opportunities, discussion forums, and bestseller lists. Try subscribing to the daily email newsletter, *TheBookseller.com Bulletin*.

- **Association of American Publishers,** publishers.org
  The homepage for this group provides myriad information on the industry, as well as statistics and links. According to the site, overall publishing sales passed the $25 *billion* mark in 2005.

- **I Want Media,** iwantmedia.com
  Founded by Patrick Phillips, a freelance writer and adjunct professor of journalism at New York University, this site features media news, resources, and industry data. It's continually updated throughout the day.

- **Booktalk,** booktalk.com
  In addition to posting articles about writing and info on literary events, this online community for book lovers features personalized author homepages. Each page contains excerpts from bestselling novels, information about upcoming releases, author biographies, and agent and publisher information.

- **Arts & Letters Daily,** aldaily.com
  As the masthead boasts, this site features articles and links covering "philosophy, aesthetics, literature, language, ideas, criticism, culture, history, music, art, trends, breakthroughs, disputes, gossip." Overwhelming? Perhaps, but this site is a great place to go if you want to see what's being covered by media outlets around the world.

BLOGS AND FORUMS

- **Gawker,** gawker.com
  A great place for media, celebrity, and New York–based gossip. You can't beat the commentary from its sardonic writers, and this site will lead you to practically every gossip site in existence. If you're into that sort of thing, that is.

- **GalleyCat,** mediabistro.com/galleycat

  A book publishing blog written by industry experts, with insider news, discussion forums, and links to other helpful resources and blogs.

Don't believe everything you Google!

Everything you read on the Internet is true, right? Wrong. Read on to find out how to tell the good stuff from the not so good.

- **Sponsored links:** When you use a search engine such as Yahoo! or Google, be wary of which links you decide to click on. The first links that pop up are usually "sponsored" links, which means that the company paid for that prime Internet real estate. Don't assume that the first links are the most reliable ones.

- **Company bias:** Some websites are biased. Shocking, we know. If a website seems to be trying to sell a product, it probably is. Be wary of sites such as these, and remember that they will say whatever they need to get you to buy something.

- **Current information:** Often websites aren't updated regularly, so, naturally, their information isn't up-to-date. Peruse all websites carefully for dates. Some websites even show a "last updated on" date on the bottom of the homepage. You wouldn't eat cheese or yogurt that was past its sell-by date, so don't trust content on websites that haven't been changed for a while.

- **Changing URLs:** Names and addresses of websites (URLs) can change as a result of the sale of a company, the sale of the URL, or a company going out of business. Watch out if you're constantly being rerouted from page to page.

- **Expertise:** When looking at a website, find out about the company behind it, usually in the "About" section. It's always good to know how much of an "expert" the mind behind the site is.

- **Beatrice,** beatrice.com

  Written by a real live published author, this book blog's primary goal is to introduce readers to writers. To wit, it features interviews with writers, short stories, author forums, author Q&As, and essays.

- **Critical Mass,** bookcriticscircle.blogspot.com
  Written by the National Book Critics Circle Board of Directors, this blog covers all things literary and critical. The posts are opinionated and sometimes controversial, but always very, very smart.

- **UnBeige,** mediabistro.com/unbeige
  A design blog written by professional designers, with a forum, links to resources and related blogs, job listings, and industry news.

66 I read maudnewton.com for smart, insightful writing about books and writers, not necessarily from a publishing perspective. It's good to read stuff that's not from a publishing perspective sometimes."

—Erin Edmison, Literary Scout
Mary Anne Thompson Associates

JOIN ORGANIZATIONS

Go ahead and be a joiner. You'll never know what you'll learn or whom you'll meet at an industry event. And your company just might pay for your membership costs down the road if you demonstrate the organization's relevance to your job.

- **Young to Publishing Group,** publishers.org/about/ypg.cfm
  A subdivision of the Association of American Publishers, YPG is a great organization for novices in the publishing field (people with fewer than five years of experience). It sponsors brown-bag lunches with guest speakers, publishes an industry newsletter, sends free advance copies to members, and hosts networking get-togethers.

- **Editorial Freelancers Association,** the-efa.org
  The EFA is a national professional organization for freelancers in the publishing industry. Its members include self-employed editors, proofreaders, copy editors, writers, researchers, and others. In addition to industry events and meetings, members benefit from an

email discussion list, a newsletter, job listings, online courses, and benefits programs.

- **Partnership in Print Production,** p3-ny.org
A joint operation between the Association of Publication Production Managers and Women in Production, P3 provides professional resources and education to professionals and students in print production, publishing, new media, and graphic communications. It sponsors educational and networking programs, including informational lunches.

- **PEN American Center,** pen.org
PEN American is a chapter of the world's oldest human rights organization and the oldest international literary organization. The organization's main goals are "to advance literature, to defend free expression, and to foster international literary fellowship," and its members include translators, writers, and editors. PEN American also offers writing grants, promotes international literature, awards literary prizes, hosts forums, and sends famous authors to inner-city public schools.

- **National Association of Women Writers,** naww.org
Dedicated to women writers, editors, and publishers, NAWW promotes community and education through events, books, CDs, and tele-events.

NETWORK

We'd all like to think that there's some kind of magic formula for getting a job. Stay in school, get good grades, work hard, build up your résumé, and, boom, you'll get a great job as soon as you start looking. We wish it were that easy. Every industry is "who-you-know," but publishing is even more so. People hop from imprint to imprint and house to house, so the sales assistant at Norton today is the sales rep at Wiley tomorrow and, maybe, someday the director of sales at Houghton Mifflin. Bottom line: Networking matters. You need to get out there, shake hands, collect business cards, and meet people. Networking involves talking to industry professionals about the job search, your résumé, and their unique career paths. When it's done well, networking leads to sage advice, new contacts, and actual job leads.

Developing a Network

Step one of networking: Go through your entire current network (i.e., everyone you know). You may think that living in Idaho with parents who are both scientists means you're SOL when it comes to publishing professionals, but you never know. Step two: Contact those professionals. Sure, it's scary to call or email someone you've never met before, but don't be afraid. You'll be surprised how many people know people who're willing to sit down and talk to a new job seeker. But you won't know anything unless you ask.

Write a quick email to your friends and family that says something like, "Hey, I'm interested in publishing. Do you happen to know anyone who works in the industry? Specifically, I'd love to talk to someone about design [or editing or insert your publishing passion here]." We promise you: Someone you know will know someone who will know someone who works in publishing or in a related field. Remember to cast a wide net: Talk to your stylist, the manager of your local bookstore, the guy your dad golfs with on the weekends, your mom's tennis partner, your high school biology teacher. Tell everyone you know that you're looking for a job in publishing.

There's another advantage to telling as many people as possible about your job hunt: You'll no doubt meet someone else who's looking for a job. You two can lean on each other as you search, sharing tidbits and information, even if you're not looking for work in the same field. What goes around comes around—you might be able to introduce your job-seeking new friend to a key contact in his industry, and he might know someone in publishing.

66 Networking is without a doubt the most critical component of a job search. Publishing is a small, insular, niche industry. Eventually everyone's paths cross. People thinking about pursuing a career in publishing can't afford to be bashful. They should be fearless about approaching friends, friends of friends, and distant relatives to seek out and find people who are already established in the publishing industry."

—**Elysa Jacobs,** Project Editor
Macmillan/McGraw-Hill

Contacting Professionals

You've got a list of people to talk to, and you know something about each name. Now what? Well, now you have to get in touch and introduce yourself. You've got a few choices for getting in touch: snail mail (boring), not care if you add her to your MySpace friends list, but someone who's been in the industry for a while (and who's a little older) might not cotton to a random person touching base in such an intimate way.

Keep these tips in mind when getting in touch with your contacts.

Consider getting your own business cards made. This way, you have something to exchange for someone else's cards.

- **Send an email.** Email's great because it's unobtrusive and easy. The downside, though, is that emails, especially emails from strangers, get deleted or go straight to the junk mail folder. Put the name of the person who referred you in the subject line, don't include any attachments, and avoid using an overly casual personal email address ("sweetiepie@aohl.com" is fine for friends, but not so fine for prospective bosses). If you don't have a professional first name. last name email address, get yourself one right now.

SAMPLE INTRODUCTORY EMAIL

TO: Sheila.Anderson@harperemail.com

FROM: Alyssa.Barton@mymail.com

SUBJECT: referred by Doug Liu

Dear Ms. Anderson:

Doug Liu highly recommended I contact you, as I have just graduated with an English degree and am interested in pursuing a publishing career. Right now, I'm trying to learn more about editorial departments at trade houses, and someday I'd like to get an editorial assistant position.

I was thrilled when I heard from Doug that you edited Hodgman's *The Areas of My Expertise*. What a hilarious and intelligent book. I'm sure you are swamped working on other great titles, but if you have a free hour, I'd enjoy very much hearing about your experiences in the publishing industry. Doug mentioned that you took a few classes at the NYU Publishing Institute; I'd love to pick your brain about whether they helped you advance. I could come by your office at your convenience, or perhaps we could meet for coffee sometime next week.

Thanks for your time and I hope to hear from you soon!

Best regards,

Alyssa Barton
917.555.5432
Alyssa.Barton@mymail.com

- **Keep it short and sweet.** Remember that you are asking someone you don't know for his or her very valuable time. Open by mentioning the name of the person who referred you in the first sentence, then go straight to the point. Now's not the time to be vague or long-winded.

> ❝ It's always easier if you don't have to cold-call the person. See if you can find a way for someone to introduce you. If that's not possible, though, flattery will always help. If you want to meet a certain editor, read some of the books he/she has published and then email a fan letter, asking if it would be possible to meet."
>
> —**Erin Edmison,** Literary Scout
> Mary Anne Thompson Associates

- **Mention what you know.** If you know the editor worked on a specific book, say so. If you know that the agent works on a specific genre, mention it. Be complimentary—and show that you've done some research.

- **Be grateful, not desperate.** Remember that you're confidently asking for their wisdom, not begging them to help you get a job. Don't forget to thank the person for his or her time.

- **Keep it professional but not stuffy.** Make an effort to sound mature and professional, as though you're already a publishing professional. But don't get cocky—you are, after all, asking a stranger for help. Again, always say "thank you."

Hanging Out at Industry Events

The biggest publishing event nationally is BookExpo America, held once a year in various cities around the country (see bookexpoamerica.com for details). Publishers, sales reps, publicists, editors, buyers, librarians, writers, and booksellers from around the world attend BEA to make deals, see what's hot, and, yes, catch up with old friends. Everybody goes from booth to booth, picking up catalogs and business cards; hearing speakers comment about the "state of the industry" and other hot topics; attending author signings; buying, selling, and negotiating for literary rights; and getting free galleys and product tie-ins (tote bags and bookmarks are especially popular). Make every effort to attend, be friendly, and don't forget to follow up with anybody you meet.

But BookExpo isn't the only worthwhile event in publishing. Far from it, in fact. Keep your ears and eyes open for book signings, book parties, or lectures and lunches hosted by publishing organizations such as Young to Publishing and the Association of American Publishers. Since you're now receiving industry newsletters such as *PW Daily* and *Publishers Lunch* (aren't you?), check out their event calendars. Mediabistro.com also hosts a plethora of free networking events for young media professionals and freelancers.

- **Introduce yourself.** Once you get yourself to an event, it may seem a little overwhelming to be surrounded by so many strangers. Feeling awkward is normal—not everyone has the power to work the room. Remind yourself of that fact, take a deep breath, and start talking to the person next to you. Ask her what kind of books she likes to read or how she heard about the event. Smile. In a few minutes, you'll be chatting like old friends. And if she's not your cup of tea, excuse yourself and go talk to someone else.

- **Collect business cards.** Whenever you meet someone new, ask for a business card. The next day, send your new pal a nice, short note over email. Say how much you enjoyed meeting the person and, if possible, mention something you discussed. If you really, truly enjoyed talking with the person, try to set up a meeting at the person's office or over coffee. Be honest: Say you're looking for a job and would love to hear more about his experiences/fall titles/sales strategies/negotiations for world rights.

- **Stay organized.** Find a way to keep track of all the business cards you collect. Note too how you met the person ("friend of Jacinda Smith"), where you met ("at Janey's birthday party"), what you talked about ("young people getting huge book contracts for first novels"), and any interesting facts about the person ("really likes Cormac McCarthy novels"). You might go old-school and use a Rolodex, or you might transfer all the info into a spreadsheet. Whichever way works for you—just don't throw the cards away!

Going on Informational Interviews

Informational interviews are just what you think they'd be. They're your chance to informally interview someone about the industry in order to get more information. They're not job interviews, and they're not your opportunity to pump someone for a job. The best informational interviews let you learn about the professional's experience and background, get advice, hear funny or interesting stories, and, hopefully, make contacts that will eventually lead to job openings. Publishing's a social industry, and people love to chat about their backgrounds and share first-job horror stories. These conversations often occur over the phone, but do your best to shoot for a face-to-face meeting.

Here are some tips for a successful informational interview.

- **Check out the company website.** Do a search on Google and *PW* to see if they've had any bestsellers or noteworthy books lately. Figure out who owns the house and who else might be under the same conglomerate's roof. Head to the bookstore or a library and flip through some titles the house has published. Write down positive comments, then try to find a way to bring up those comments during your meeting: "I really liked the jacket you designed for *Klimt: A Life*. Could you talk to me about the creative process behind that project?"

- **Research the specific person you're interviewing.** As always, Google is your friend. See what comes up in relation to the person you're interviewing with, and maybe use that info to your advantage. Googling people is an open secret—everybody does it—but some people still get creeped out, so be careful how you bring up whatever you've learned. Saying, "I know you worked on the Klimt project. What was that like?" is one thing; saying, "So, you were the arm-wrestling champion of your sorority," is another.

66 Nothing is more flattering than a person who takes the time to know a company's history and product line. I recommend checking out the 'What's New' areas on websites and press releases. For instance, see if they are launching a new product line and give some helpful insights about their product. Older editors are especially interested in the ways younger people are buying things . . . anything, because bookselling is becoming very creative and tech driven."

—Emerson John Probst, Senior Editor
Marketplace Books

- **Be cool.** You don't want to be so organized that you come off like a stiff, unfun robot. Instead, be relaxed during your meeting. Let topics come up naturally rather than asking questions rapid-fire. Act as if you're very content with your life and want to share that contentment with others, but don't be arrogant. Do not act desperate. Do not panic. Do not say, "Please get me a job at Scribner. I'll do anything, including shining the CEO's shoes. Please. Plllleeeeaaaassseeee."

- **Prepare but don't overprepare.** Bring a copy of your résumé and know what you want to talk about. Memorize a little spiel about yourself, specifically about who you are and why you're taking up this person's time. (It's okay to just repeat the first few lines of your email.) If you're not clear about why you want to meet with that specific person, you're not ready for an informational interview.

- **Ask good questions.** Who doesn't enjoy talking about themselves? Nobody, that's who. Don't forget that it's your job to put the "interview" in informational interview. Here are a few good questions to get you started:

    » *What's your typical day like?*
    » *What do you enjoy most about your job?*

> » *What you do wish someone had told you when you were just starting out?*
>
> » *If you could do it all again, would you do anything differently?*
>
> » *What do you love most about your job? What do you hate?*
>
> » *What's the one thing you wish you'd known about publishing before you began your career?*

Another great way to find out about what a publishing house is like is to set up an informational interview with the house's human resources department.

- **Be gracious and polite.** During the interview, sit back, listen, learn, take notes, and respond to what the person is saying. At the end, say thank you, shake his hand, and get a business card. When you get home, rewrite your notes while the interview is still fresh in your mind. (Definitely take notes: Just like everyone likes answering questions about his background, everyone likes to feel as if his comments are worth being recorded by a young job seeker.) Write down any other leads that you'd like to follow after going on that interview or more questions that you want answered later. Finally, don't forget to send the person a thank-you note.

Staying in Touch (Without Stalking)

So you've made some contacts, gotten some business cards, and had a few informational interviews. What next? Stay in touch, silly. Initial meetings aren't enough: You need to touch base once every few months. You never know when one of your contacts might have a job lead or opening or when someone you know might know someone whom you must meet. Don't email them every week, obviously, but do touch base once in a while—when you have a question, of course, as well as when you have news.

❝ Every informational interview is different. While I could tell some people simply agreed to lend me some of their time because they promised a colleague, others were extremely helpful. One woman marked up my résumé and gave me a sample of her husband's as a guide. I also contacted previous coworkers of mine and asked if I could meet with them for a quick cup of coffee. They always said yes."

—Lindsay Weiskittel, Editorial Assistant
Spark Publishing/Barnes & Noble

> **Memorable mentors**
>
> Once you've talked up your interest to your friends and family and gone on a few informational interviews, you may find yourself bonding with one professional in particular. This person might have a career you'd like to emulate, or he might just be someone in publishing that's easy to talk to and generous with his own experiences. That's great—you've found yourself a mentor. Your relationship doesn't have to be official. No matter what, don't say something like, "Will you be my mentor?" Instead, just be glad that you've found someone you like, trust, enjoy spending time with, and feel comfortable asking for advice. Definitely stay in touch with that person more regularly than you would your other contacts, and let him know how things are going on your end.

CONSIDER FURTHER EDUCATION

After doing all this research and talking, you might find that you need more education in order to really make it in publishing. Keep in mind, though, that going back to school will not only cost you in dollars but also in time: While you're toiling away in the stacks, your publishing cohorts will be climbing the corporate ladder. Also, publishing is very much an apprenticeship industry where established professionals teach newbies the ropes for several years until the newbies are ready to be promoted. So is it worth it to go back to school? It's up to you.

Go Back to School if . . .

- **You don't have a bachelor's degree.** Nearly all jobs in publishing require a four-year college degree.

- **You have a degree, but it's not at all related to the publishing industry.** For instance, you majored in engineering, took no liberal arts classes, and have zero experience in publishing. Sometimes having an advanced degree gives you a boost, as when an editor in educational publishing has a master's in education.

- **You don't have the skills necessary for the publishing job you're looking for.** If you're a designer, say, you'll need to be a desktop-publishing master. Taking some classes and getting a degree might be worth it if you need specific skills, but remember too that people in publishing definitely learn on the job.

- **You don't have the expertise necessary for the types of books you want to work on.** Say you want to do production on science books. If you don't know anything about science, you best get yourself back to school for a brush-up.

- **You have the time, money, and desire.** Many schools offer publishing programs, at the end of which you receive a certification in publishing. What you're essentially paying for with these programs is the opportunity to network with people in the industry and the chance to quickly learn a little about all the various departments.

PUBLISHING PROGRAMS

So you need a BA or BS to work in publishing, but few schools let you major in publishing. What to do, what to do? If you want to go back to school specifically for publishing, you have a few options:

- Get a master of science in publishing
- Take some courses in publishing
- Attend a publishing program

Pace University (pace.edu) and the School of Continuing and Professional Studies at New York University (scps.nyu.edu) both offer the MS in Publishing. At either school, you'll choose from an array of courses such as Principles of Publishing, Editorial Principles and Practice, Cookbook Copyediting, and The Business of Business-to-Business Publishing.

Although some professionals certainly have a master's in publishing, it's more common to either take a few courses or attend a publishing program, which usually culminates in a certificate. Mediabistro.com offers courses around the country, and NYU lets you take individual courses in its publishing program. You can even earn a certificate in editing, publishing, or business-to-business publishing there. Once you're hired as an entry-level assistant, your company might offer to send you to a class so that you can learn some skills quickly.

The last option—attending a program—is great for people with little to no industry experience. You'll get the opportunity to network with the program's teachers, who work in publishing; do an internship or two; hang out with other young job seekers; and hear about the various departments of a publishing house. Programs usually last between a month and six weeks, and they generally cover both magazine and book publishing. At the end, you'll receive a certificate and help with the job search (some programs sponsor career fairs). The downside is cost: These programs don't come cheap, so weigh the pros and cons. Here's a list of some of the best programs in New York.

- **The Columbia Publishing Course,** www.jrn.columbia.edu/academic_programs/publishing/
  This six-week intensive summer program offers a certificate of completion at the course's end. Held in the Columbia University School of Journalism, the program is divided into three parts. First, you'll learn the ins and outs of book publishing. Second, you'll examine magazine publishing. Finally, you'll study electronic publishing and new media, particularly its impact on the publishing industry.

- **The Publishing Certificate Program at the City College of New York,** www.ccny.cuny.edu/publishing_certificate/course.html
  Founded by bestselling author Walter Mosley, this program attempts to increase diversity in publishing, as well as teach its attendees about how publishing houses function and make books. The program will also hook you up with an internship at BookExpo or at a house. In addition to classes on book publishing, you can take electives such as Print Production and Typography.

- **New York University Summer Publishing Institute,** scps.nyu.edu/departments/department.jsp?deptId=14
  This six-week intensive program at the Center for Publishing is divided into two sections: The first half deals with magazine publishing, and the second half with book publishing. SPI focuses on the entire process of book production, marketing, and distribution, as well as multimedia publishing. The program also pays special attention to career planning; it hosts panels, discussions, and a job fair.

Don't Go Back to School if . . .

- **You're still not 100 percent sure publishing is the industry for you.** Decide first by talking to more people, going on informational interviews, and doing internships.

- **You already have a bachelor's degree in any liberal arts field,** especially English, literature, history, or journalism.

- **You'll mind being a little older than your cohorts.** Think carefully if you want to go to grad school: It's not always easy to return to an industry once you've left, and you might not feel totally cool being a 26-year-old editorial assistant or sales assistant with a master's degree.

- **You just can't afford it right now.** There are plenty of ways you can continue to learn about the industry and gain the skills you need without paying for classes right now. If you're certain you'll need them down the road, start saving money now so you can take classes later.

- **You'd rather learn on the job.** Remember that you can always take a course or two here and there to learn a computer program or to brush up on your editing. Courses are a great way to gain knowledge without making a major cost or time commitment.

Evaluating Schools

Remember that your ultimate goal is to get a job in publishing, so make sure that the school is well equipped to help you land that job. Here are a few things to think about when you're trying to find the right school:

- **Class content:** Do they teach what you need to learn?
- **Faculty:** Do the faculty members have years of experience in their field?
- **Degree:** Do they offer the degree you need?
- **Job placement:** Where do their alumni work after they graduate? Does the job placement continue after you've graduated?
- **Affordability:** Do they offer financial assistance?
- **Flexibility:** Do they offer night classes? Weekend classes? Online courses?
- **Internship:** Do they have internship opportunities with publishing companies?

Paying for School

Need a financial boost? Believe it or not, there are tons of resources for getting money to help you pay for higher education.

- **Scholarships and grants:** Do some online and library research on local business, corporations, and philanthropists who offer scholarships and grants.

- **The school:** Many schools offer scholarships and grants; all you need to do is ask! The financial aid office will have information on how to apply for them.

- **Work-study and on-campus employment:** Working at the school may lower your tuition or waive it completely. Find out more from the financial aid office.

Dollars and sense

The government offers the following tuition resources:

- Federal Pell Grant (limited to undergraduates)
- Federal Perkins Loan
- Federal Supplemental Educational Opportunity Grant (limited to undergraduates)
- Stafford Loan
- Subsidized FFEL or Direct Loan

For details on qualifications and applications for these resources, go to the U.S. Department of Education's Federal Student Aid at a Glance website at studentaid.ed.gov/students/publications/student_guide/2005-2006/english/glance.htm.

5

INTERNING

Interning gives you the chance to actually practice a job. An internship lets you test the publishing waters before you dive in, ride a publishing bike with training wheels, walk before you run in the publishing race . . . you get the point. We can't stress this enough: Do an internship. It's so important that we're going to repeat ourselves in bold with exclamation points: **Get yourself a publishing internship!!!** You'll not only get a chance to see what you like (and don't like) about publishing through an internship, but you'll also get to pump up your résumé and make valuable contacts.

DEFINE THE INTERNSHIP

Okay, so an internship is an opportunity for you to really see what it's like to be in publishing, specifically whether the company and department for which you intern is right for you. As you start to think about where you might want to work, be open to different experiences and be open to the possibility that you're actually better suited for a different company or department than you might originally have thought. Say you've always had your heart set on working in marketing for a huge house. Well, an internship lets you see whether that's a worthwhile endeavor or whether you're better off doing design for an independent. You'll never know unless you try.

As an intern, you'll probably receive a tiny, tiny salary (about enough to cover your subway fare, but just barely). So you won't be doing it for the money. Instead, you'll be doing it for the experience, the on-the-job training, and the contacts. Keep that in mind as you start looking and planning. You may be spending more time at the copy machine and by the coffeemaker than around books, but the potential payoff makes these mindless chores worth it.

> **Internships aren't just for college students . . .**
>
> They're opportunities for individuals to learn more about an industry, regardless of whether you're still in school. Sure, as an intern, you'll have to give up the possibilities of a 401(k), spending money, and health insurance, which your fellow graduates will get at their first jobs, but you'll gain experience—and that will make you that much more marketable when it comes time to get your first job.

LEARN WHAT TO EXPECT

In publishing, you have to pay your dues to move up—that's what it means to work in an industry with an apprenticeship model. You start low, toil away for a couple of years, and then slowly get promoted up the ladder. This isn't just some BS about paying your dues. You'll only get promoted once you've spent a couple years toiling away as an assistant. As much as making coffee and filing contracts might not appeal to you, starting with the menial tasks is the only way to get ahead. Be realistic about what you'll do as an intern: You'll be cleaning up files, not designing book jackets; taking notes at meetings, not running the meetings; sitting in on sales calls, not making them yourself; and so on.

The tasks in every department are pretty much the same across the board. Generally, interns do administrative work such as answering phones, updating schedules in Excel, and distributing mail—the same sorts of tasks that entry-level assistants perform. Here's a brief overview of what an internship in each department might be like.

Editorial Internships

As an intern, you might not feel as if you're having any impact on the process of acquiring, developing, or editing a book. Not so. Publishing houses function like machines, and every cog counts. Remind yourself of this as you're:

- Copying manuscripts
- Mailing materials—including manuscripts, ARCs, and galleys—to authors, agents, or possible blurb contributors
- Reviewing unsolicited manuscripts and mailing refusal letters (i.e., dealing with the slush pile)
- Answering phones
- Helping prepare manuscript files for production (accepting editors' changes using Microsoft Word, for example)
- Writing readers' reports (wherein you evaluate a manuscript)
- Managing, copying, and filing contracts

66 Get over yourself! It's perfectly natural—and, in fact, largely procedural—to start 'at the bottom' doing routine tasks like mailing, database maintenance, faxing, and filing. It's not demeaning work at all—someone has to do it, and that someone is you. Keep your eyes and ears open and you will learn a LOT in a short amount of time, and you'll move up!"

—**Arija Weddle,** Agent's Assistant, Agent-in-Training
The Nicholas Ellison Agency

Production/Manufacturing Internships

Here, you'll get to see what actually goes into making a book. Expect to engage in a lot of detail-related work, including:

- Checking blues to make sure the printer hasn't made an error
- Transferring the author's corrections onto the set of pages with the proofreader's corrections
- Proofreading cover and interior proofs
- Routing materials to other departments
- Preparing files to send to the typesetter
- Sending materials, such as setting manuscript or proofs, to the typesetter or sending materials to freelancers
- Doing light copyediting

Design Internships

We'll be honest: Design internships are rare. If you do snag one, you'll probably be:

- Answering the phone
- Saving files into new formats and making PDFs
- Copying and printing interiors and covers
- Trafficking materials through other departments
- Helping the designers keep track of projects by making schedules
- Reviewing typeset pages to make sure specs were followed
- Laying out books based on templates that the designers have provided (if you're lucky and you've been there awhile)

Marketing/Publicity Internships

An internship in this department will let you see how marketing materials and publicists generate buzz about titles. While your buzz might not be particularly loud as an intern, you'll contribute to the company's collective hum by:

- Helping to maintain databases, mailing lists, and sales records
- Printing and collating materials
- Preparing press kits and publicity mailings (sending out ARCs, organizing materials into folders, attaching labels, and so on)
- Organizing and filing press clippings of book reviews
- Sending form letters to book reviewers and potential blurb contributors
- Writing press releases
- Helping manage author tours

Sales Internships

As a sales intern, you'll be helping the in-house sales staff move books by:

- Sending out sales materials, including the catalog, to sales reps
- Maintaining and updating a database of sales targets
- Tracking sales reps in the field
- Helping to prepare sales reports

6 6 Publishing can sound very glamorous to people who don't know much about it. But job seekers need to realize that there's still a lot of paper pushing and bureaucracy, as at any company. The majority of us don't sit around in our sweats editing the Great American Novel, with a cup of joe on the table and Fido asleep beside us. That said, publishing is fascinating and satisfying."

—Rebecca J. Ortman, Market Research Analyst
Pearson Longman English Language Training

GET AN INTERNSHIP

Sadly, a great internship won't just materialize if you say "please." Snagging an opportunity with a well-known company involves some planning and research. First, you'll need to decide which companies to target, and then you'll need to create a plan of action. Applying for and getting an internship takes work, but it's good practice for when you're applying for—and hopefully getting—your first job.

Figuring Out Where You Want to Be

Your first step to securing a dream internship is to consider your options. Since an internship is probably only for a semester or summer, feel free to apply to jobs that sound kind of interesting. You never know what might float your boat, so be open to various possibilities. Consider location, department, size of company, and length of internship. Don't be afraid to take a chance!

START WITH WHAT YOU KNOW (OR DON'T KNOW)

Let's start easy. Make a list of all the places you'd like to work. Then do some research to see what's available to you (later in this chapter we give you a list of some of the most prestigious internship programs out there). Here are a few guidelines to help you narrow down your options:

- **Size matters.** Small companies offer more opportunities for you to experience the inner workings of a house. Such varied experience does mean greater responsibility and perhaps more challenges, but these things also make internships in smaller companies more difficult to obtain (plus, small companies generally only hire one or two interns at a time). Bigger companies are more corporate and have name recognition, so competition for internships there can be intense too. At the same time, though, an internship at a big house will have a somewhat higher turnover, so there will be more opportunities to apply.

- **Choose your books.** You won't enjoy your job if you don't like the books you're working on. Think about what books you like to read and the type of books you pick up off the shelf at a bookstore. Carefully consider too the audience for these books, as well as the type of people who usually write the books. You'll hate life if you're stuck working with and for people whose interests vastly differ from yours.

- **Choose your part.** Examine the different departments and determine where you might fit best (go back to chapter 2 if you need a refresher). Competition for internships in editorial and design tends to be greater than for those in other departments. Editorial and design demand creativity, while production and manufacturing require someone who's detailed oriented, sales requires a self-starter who can smooth-talk her way out of any situation, and marketing/publicity needs outgoing people who love to spread their enthusiasm. But again, don't be afraid to take a risk and go for an internship in a department you don't know very much about. You might discover a hidden passion.

- **Consider dollars.** Whether you should be looking for a paid internship depends on your unique circumstances. Some great internships that might lead to excellent opportunities come with a tiny or nonexistent stipend. In other words, can you live on savings for a while? If you need to get a part-time job, are you sure that working at the job won't interfere with the internship? When looking at unpaid internships, make sure that the exposure, opportunities, and networking potential make up for the free labor.

- **Location, location.** Although New York offers the most internship opportunities, this city's not your only option. University presses and small houses can be found everywhere; check out *Literary Market Place* for the names of all publishers across the United States. And broaden your search to include literary agencies and book packagers that aren't necessarily in New York.

Application Timeline

Researching and applying for internships takes a while. As you'll see below, it's a good idea to start approximately six or so months in advance to guarantee plenty of time to check out companies and departments, prepare your résumé, practice interviewing, apply, and interview. This timeline's designed for upper-class college students, but you can use it as a gauge no matter where you are in school or in the internship-application process. Just remember: It takes time to do it right!

FALL SEMESTER (SEPTEMBER–NOVEMBER)

- Develop your résumé.
- Talk to recent graduates about their internship experiences.
- Begin researching companies where you might like to intern.
- Check out your college's credit program: Will doing an internship delay your time to degree?

WINTER VACATION

- Make a list of books you enjoy, then do some research on the companies that publish those books.
- Get online and do a search for "publishing internships."
- Research specific companies for which you'd like to work (again).
- Put together a tracking sheet with opportunities, contact info, and deadlines (see our sample on page 143).
- Plan for some informational interviews.

SAMPLE INTERNSHIP TRACKING SHEET

Date	Company	Contact name	Contact Info	Activity	Next Step
2/10	Random House	Tonya Reedy	treedy@rrhouse.com	Emailed résumé	Call 2/15
2/15	HarperCollins	Marcus Sheer	(212) 555-1852 msheer@hacollins.com	Emailed résumé	Call 2/20
2/28	New Press	Nancy Engels	(917) 555-2210 nancy@npress.com	Left voice mail	Email 3/5
3/1	Quirk Press	Dana Fairbanks	(212) 555-7770	Applied online	Call 3/6
3/9	Penguin	Alison Curry	acurry@penguin.com	Applied online	Send references; set up interview
3/19	Ecco	Willa Smith	(718) 555-1234	Left voice mail	call 4/1
3/19	Doubleday/ Broadway	—	—	checked website	check again 4/1

SPRING SEMESTER (FEBRUARY–MARCH)

- Finalize your résumé.
- Print 20 copies of your résumé on good-quality paper.
- Make sure you have a "plain text" résumé to send in the body of an email (the fancy formatting that looks good on paper often turns to gibberish over email).
- Go on the informational interviews you set up back in January.
- Ask faculty members and former employers for letters of recommendation if necessary.
- Meet with your career center advisers for access to job boards.
- Attend internship fairs hosted by your school or by outside companies.
- Check out online internship services.
- Apply for internships, keeping your tracking sheet updated.
- Have a great interview (or two, or six . . .).
- Write thank-you notes.
- Get the internship!

Finding and Applying for Internships

Most publishing companies have spots for interns—that's the good news. The bad news is that lots and lots of people covet those spots, so you have to work hard to find an internship that's right for you. Utilize your network and your career center, and don't be afraid to cold-call companies to see what's what. You'll also need to be a thorough and persistent researcher, using everything from Google to *PW* to message boards to your favorite books to dig up leads. Above all, don't forget to do the following.

- **Network.** You never know who might have a well-placed friend or relative at Bantam, Ballantine, Copper Canyon, or some other house for which you'd like to work. Get in touch with your family, friends, neighbors, old teachers, old roommates, old soccer coaches, and anyone else you can think of to say that you're looking for an internship. And don't forget about all the people with whom you had informational interviews. Dig out those business cards, and drop everyone a friendly email that says something like, "I'm looking for an internship in sales. Might you know of any opportunities?"

Talk to former interns

You can find out a lot about internships by talking to people who've interned. They'll have the inside scoop about how to find internships, how to make the most out of your internship, whether to take an internship that doesn't pay, and what to watch out for at a particular company. Plus, talking to former interns lets you expand your network even if you're all working in different industries. If you're in publishing, it definitely doesn't hurt to have friends who work for magazines, newspapers, law firms, and advertising agencies. Once you're all ensconced in your first jobs, you never know who might have a great idea or contact that could lead to a bestseller or cool design down the road. Your college career center probably has a list of former interns who'd be willing to talk to someone just starting out.

- **Use school resources.** Your college career center no doubt maintains internship/job boards, holds internship fairs, and invites companies to campus. These events are usually open to current students and alumni. Attend, bringing along many copies of your résumé and a big smile. The career center probably also subscribes to online databases for intern wannabes; sign up and log on. You'll also want to get on listservs run by your major's department: Employers sometimes contact academic departments directly for referrals, so make sure to let professors and career counselors know that you're available and looking for work.

- **Talk to alums.** If your school has an active alumni association or mentoring program, get in touch with people who already work in publishing. Who wouldn't want to help out a fellow Blue Devil or Commodore?

- **Hit the 'net.** Publishing internships are all over the web. Individual companies often post opportunities on their homepages, and you can find further job listings on Craigslist or Monster.com. In addition, your college might subscribe to a password-protected subscription site, which can send you targeted postings. You could also consider buying access to such a site. But wait, does anyone even call it "the 'net" anymore?

Recommended Publishing Internships Websites

- » bookjobs.com/internships.php
- » cbcbooks.org/careers/internships.html
- » mediabistro.com/joblistings
- » publishingcentral.com
- » internshipprograms.com
- » jobsearchsite.com
- » newyork.craigslist.org

- **Check out established programs.** Some of the big houses sponsor their own fancy internship programs. Open to juniors, seniors, and graduate students, these programs generally run for 12 to 14 weeks during the summer. They give participants a chance to see how lots of different departments work since most programs force you to spend a little time in several different areas of the house. They also require you to attend lunchtime talks with higher-ups in the industry, so you'll get to network while you work. Here are few names of and links to some of the biggies:

  - » **Scholastic Children's Defense Fellows Program,** scholastic.com/aboutscholastic/job/defensefund.htm
  - » **Random House Summer Internship Program,** careers.randomhouse.com/wms/bmhr/index.php?ci=3934
  - » **HarperCollins Summer Internship Program,** harpercollinscareers.com/careers/students/st_internships.html
  - » **Simon & Schuster Summer Internship Program,** www.simonsays.com/content/feature.cfm?sid=33&feature_id=1785

But the big houses also offer programs for recent graduates. These programs are long—usually over a year—and they're highly competitive. But if you get in, your chances of getting a full-time job at the end are really high. Some programs, such as Simon & Schuster's, put you into one department for a year, but others, such as the Random House program, will rotate you from department to department, giving you a taste of all aspects of publishing. If you're out of school and you're sure publishing's for you, consider applying to one of these programs:

> » **Random House Associates Program,**
>   careers.randomhouse.com/wms/bmhr/index.php?ci=3930
> » **HarperCollins Rotational Associates Program,**
>   harpercollinscareers.com/careers/careers/display_jobs.
>   asp?id=rotat_prog
> » **Simon & Schuster Associates Program,**
>   www.simonsays.com/content/feature.cfm?sid=33&feature_id=3174

- **Apply far and wide.** Don't limit your options this early in the game by only applying for one or two spots. Instead, spread your net far and wide. Don't put all your eggs in one internship basket. Don't set your heart on one and not apply to another. (Could we have any more clichés in this paragraph?) Basically, don't wait to hear from one company before you apply to another. You may have your heart set on working at Delacorte, but so do lots and lots of other people. It takes human resources a while to go through all the résumés and decide whom they want to interview. Use that time to apply elsewhere.

- **Create your own internship.** Okay, we'll admit it: This is something of a long shot. That said, there's no reason why you can't call up the human resources department at a place you'd like to work and offer your services for free. Some companies don't have official internship programs, but they would probably welcome interns. Make sure you're very specific and organized when you propose yourself as a DIY intern: Tell the company how many hours you plan to work a week, what department you'd like to work in, and what you hope to learn from the internship. At the very least, you'll get experience selling yourself as a viable candidate—and you might score an informational interview out of it.

- **Follow the three cardinal rules of job applications.** They're very simple, but you'd be surprised at how many people flub these basic steps:

1. Make sure you meet the minimum qualifications.
2. Follow the directions *exactly* as posted.
3. Submit your application on time.

66 I spent one summer as an intern at Charlesbridge Publishing in Watertown, Massachusetts. It was an invaluable experience. Not only did it allow me to observe and participate in the day-to-day responsibilities of an editor, it also gave me tremendous insight into the types of publishing (trade vs. educational) that I wanted to seek out (or avoid at all costs) when it was time to apply for full-time positions. The internship validated my beliefs that I wanted to pursue a career in publishing books for children."

—**Elysa Jacobs,** Project Editor
Macmillan/McGraw-Hill

Comparing Opportunities

Resist the temptation to take the first internship that's offered to you. And don't take an internship just because it pays well. If you've followed our advice (and you have, haven't you?), you probably cast a wide net. Who knows what kinds of offers you might receive in the next few weeks? Be patient, and compare the internship offers you receive *before* deciding on one to do.

At the end of the day, it's your call whether to take or pass on an internship. Say you apply for an editorial internship at Dell, but the human resources department at Bertelsmann only offers you a production internship at Harlem Moon. Should you take it? On the one hand, you'd be working for an imprint owned by the same company as the one you originally wanted to work for—and you might be able to network you way into another opportunity at the end of your internship. On the other hand, you'd be working in production rather than editorial. Could you last a summer of doing work you're not really that interested in? (For the record, we'd probably take the Harlem Moon internship simply because Bertelsmann runs Random House, and, well, Random House is Random House.) Trust your instincts, but consider the following as you compare opportunities.

- **The boss and the crew:** Hopefully, you got a good feeling about your boss during the interview. Otherwise, it could be a very, *very* long summer. In the best internships, someone is specifically assigned to serve as your mentor. They guide you through the procedures, answer questions, and introduce you to important people in other departments.

- **The books and the audience:** If you like the company's books, you're more likely to enjoy working there. Even if you're not necessarily interested in reading the books yourself, you should have a familiarity with the type of people who do read them. Don't accept an internship with a scholarly publisher if you absolutely abhor highbrow nonfiction, dissertations, and the like.

- **Convenience and money:** Location is a huge a factor here. Are you going to have to spend a long time in the car, on a bus, or on a subway? If you have to move to another city in order to accept the position, will you be able to find a place to stay? (Most companies don't provide housing for their interns.) If the internship is unpaid, make sure you can afford to make little or no money for the summer. The truth is, some people can, and some people can't. Talk it through with your family and consider your budget very carefully.

- **Your long-term goals:** Where you end up often depends on where you begin. Think about the books you'd like to be working on in the long run. If you intern with a children's book small press, you'll have an easier time selling yourself to Scholastic. If you have a dream company in mind but can't land a position there, choose a publisher that makes similar books so that you're more competitive next time around.

- **The perks:** Sometimes the fringe benefits make all the difference, like a company cafeteria or paid parking or the availability of free books. Maybe you've always wanted to live in New York City or you like idea of being able to say you're interning at Nan A. Talese. These perks could mean a heck of a lot more than money in your pocket.

I had an internship selling ad space for a regional wedding magazine. That experience was mostly cold calling. While I realized I did not want a career in sales, I did learn something about perseverance as well as office etiquette. In addition, I was exposed to the corporate culture of publishing, which I liked."

—**Francine Rosado-Cruz,** HR Diversity Manager
Penguin Group (USA)

SUCCEED AS AN INTERN (OR NOT)

Bravo! You've landed your internship. Jump up and down, call your friends, buy a new outfit, and shout your successes from a rooftop. Then, when you've calmed down, read our suggestions for making sure you *keep* that internship—and maybe earn a shot at a full-time position.

10 Ways to Impress Your Employer

1. **Show up.** Be there on time, every day, ready to work and looking pretty. No sweatsuits. No smoke breath.

2. **Be courteous.** Be respectful too.

3. **Listen and absorb.** There's a lot going on, so pay attention.

4. **Cheerfully accept all assignments, no matter how boring.** Make coffee as if you were acquiring a manuscript; file papers as if you were selling books to libraries.

5. **Participate when asked.** And refrain from second-guessing any of your superiors.

6. **Be proactive.** Ask how you can help out, and promptly tell your supervisor when you're finished with an assignment and ready to take on new tasks.

If you're still in school, don't forget to find out if you can receive academic credit for your internship. Make sure your paperwork is completed accurately—no internship's worth the shock of not being able to graduate on time.

7. **Limit lunch to lunchtime.** While you're at it, keep your personal business out of the workplace.

8. **Fulfill your commitment.** Don't leave two weeks early because you've got too much schoolwork.

9. **Ask questions.** Whenever you have an opportunity to do so, politely ask for more information. Don't be annoying, but try to get more information whenever possible.

10. **Find a mentor.** If the company doesn't assign you someone to work alongside, interest yourself in what others are doing, and your work relationships will grow.

66 If you're smart, you're reading all the memos you're filing and you're paying attention to the catalog copy you're faxing. By paying a little extra attention, you'll learn a lot."

—**Colleen Schwartz,** Senior Publicist
St. Martin's Press

10 Ways to Lose Your Internship (and Any Chance of Working for the Company in the Future!)

Sometimes good students get good internships and lose them. There are things you just can't do at work, even if you feel absolutely entitled to, so don't . . .

1. **Cry.** 'Nuff said.

2. **Arrive late.** Figure out the traffic patterns, the subway schedule, etc.—whatever you need in order to be early.

3. **Develop an attitude.** Your employer knows when you're silently fuming, "I forked over too much money for college to be packing manila envelopes with galleys."

4. **Call your employer an hour after you're supposed to be in to say you're sick.** If you really can't make it to work, call your boss before her day begins.

5. **Call in sick more than once.** Unless you're absolutely, horribly sick and contagious, get your bottom to work every day. And if you are practically dying, be prepared to show your employers a note.

6. **Take home anything that belongs to the company.** Leave the Post-Its and envelopes at work. Don't even think about taking office supplies, free books, or anything else.

7. **Tell tales from the trenches.** What happens at the office, stays at the office. Don't even *think* about starting a "My First Internship" blog. Full-fledged employees have been fired for less. You'll probably even have to sign a confidentiality agreement before you start your internship, so by all means, don't breach it.

8. **Bad-mouth anyone in the company or anyone at a competing company.** The golden rule? Don't bad-mouth anyone at all.

9. **Be embarrassed to ask for clarification.** Your boss would much rather explain something twice than have you screw up something even once.

10. **Speak your mind without thinking.** You may want to offer your two cents, but make sure you are asked for your opinion before speaking up. Respect your elders, particularly their seniority as publishing professionals.

EXPLORE ALTERNATIVES TO INTERNING

Sometimes, no matter how well you plan, you don't land the internship you want. Luckily for you, there are plenty of other good opportunities out there to learn about and observe the publishing industry.

- **Work at a bookstore.** Getting a job at a bookstore is relatively easy, and working at a bookstore is the next-best thing to having experience at an actual publishing company. You'd be surprised how much you can learn just being around books a few hours a day and watching what people buy.

- **Work at a school publication.** Whether it be the yearbook, newspaper, or literary magazine, any publishing experience is a big plus on your résumé, even if it isn't book publishing. Many of the skills you acquire—desktop publishing, editing, writing, layout—are just as crucial in the world of books. Truth be told, you should probably do this even if you do get a spectacular internship.

- **Work at a library.** Much like working at a bookstore, a library is another opportunity to be surrounded by books. Not only will you become more and more familiar with what types of books people are checking out, but libraries are also full of publications and electronic resources for your learning pleasure.

- **Work at an office.** Since most internships and entry-level jobs in publishing are highly administrative, having experience in this area can definitely earn you a second glance. If you can't land your dream internship, get your foot in the door by doing administrative work at a publishing company, newspaper, or magazine. You can start building internal contacts if you take a temp job or work as a receptionist. This may seem like a long, roundabout way to go, but many bosses come to really care for great administrative assistants and are happy to serve as references for future jobs. Admin work is also a great opportunity to get a broad overview of the way a company works.

- **Teach or tutor.** Become a tutor or volunteer to help teach creative writing or reading to elementary school students. Teaching experience shows a love of knowledge for its own sake that wins points with publishing companies, especially if you choose to work for a children's or educational publisher.

- **Volunteer.** Who doesn't love free help? If you're interested in book production or design, why not try a hand at designing pamphlets, flyers, demo covers, newsletters, or invitations for friends and family? Do it for free to sharpen your skills and build a portfolio. Or volunteer at a publishing company, helping out with anything from sorting mail to shelving books.

- **Try again.** If at first you don't succeed—or if you waited until the very last minute—try again. While we don't recommend waiting until the end of the semester to find an internship, sometimes procrastinators get lucky. If you're desperate, try contacting the human resources departments of publishing houses where you'd like to work. Check in, and mention that you're still available. You never know who might have dropped out or canceled at the last minute, leaving a space open. And then make a vow to yourself to start earlier next year.

6

GETTING A JOB

S kills: check. Résumé: check. Internship: check. Diploma: check. Looks like you're ready to get yourself a full-time job. But getting that job involves more than just fancy résumé paper and a sharp new suit from Banana Republic. You need to figure out where the jobs are. You need to do some research, network, apply, and interview. Don't worry: We'll show you exactly what you need to do to find yourself a first job that truly rocks.

RESEARCH YOUR OPTIONS

It's great to have a dream job in mind, but you'll also want to do some research into what else might be out there. To begin, you'll need to find the job postings. Is Coffee House Press hiring? Does Soho Press even have an opening for an editorial assistant? Does the marketing/publicity team at HarperCollins handle all the imprints, or does each imprint have its own marketing/publicity team? Once you've found the postings, you need to learn everything there is to know about the companies before you can even think about applying.

Finding Job Postings

Publishing always has entry-level jobs. Trouble is, publishing also has tons of eager beavers like yourself who'll willingly work long hours for low pay as assistants. Before you lose heart, though, remember that the jobs have to be found before they get filled—and we're gonna show you exactly how to find them.

ONLINE JOB BOARDS
Here's where the publishing jobs are on the Internet, so check these sites religiously.

- **Publishers Lunch Job Board,** publishersmarketplace.com/jobs
Hands down the best online resource for the industry—and not just for job openings. Make sure you subscribe to *Publishers Lunch,* the daily newsletter, and consider forking up the extra $20 a month to get complete access to the site.

- **Bookjobs.com**
A great e-resource targeted specifically to college students and recent college graduates, as well as to young people already in the industry but without a ton of experience. Bookjobs has a searchable database to help you find the right job, and the site includes internship listings and tools for matching your college major to different publishing positions.

- **Mediabistro.com,** mediabistro.com/joblistings
The most popular website for media jobs. It has a very user-friendly searchable job list, which lets you narrow your search by industry and location. There's also a ton of resources available for facilitating your job hunt and making you a more desirable candidate, ranging from networking events to panel discussions to seminars and classes.

- **Publishers Weekly,** jobs.publishersweekly.com
The online companion to the must-read trade magazine. Its job board isn't searchable, but it stays current, and the site has other valuable resources such as a sales calendar (which lets you know which titles are going on sale when).

Last, don't forget to search your college job boards. Many companies list directly with schools, sometimes posting jobs that can't be found on their own websites or through the public job boards.

WHAT WANT ADS TELL YOU (AND WHAT THEY DON'T)
Sales assistant wanted to work at big, impersonal media conglomerate. You'll get your very own desk, but you'll have to share a cubicle with two other assistants (one of whom loves, loves, loves garlic). There's no window either.

Crappy pay, long hours, some benefits. Duties include photocopying, answering the phone, and coping with a boss going through a messy divorce, who's also trying to lose fifteen pounds and quit smoking. Must be able to multitask and simultaneously lick butts of two high-maintenance, egocentric sociopaths who like to call themselves sales reps. Mmmmm. Tasty.

Oh, if only all job ads were so honest. Want ads give you the basics: job title, primary responsibilities, and requisite skills. The ad will also state the name of the company, explain how to apply, and give you some sense of the benefits or pay. Job ads won't tell you any of the juicy details such as perks, salary, potential for advancement, or job culture. You'll have to find all that out on your own. Here's where your network comes in: Call up Jesse Jones from the Mediabistro.com party you went to and ask her how she likes working at Harlequin. The interview, should you make it that far, is another opportunity for you to see what's what.

Regularly take a look at the want ads, even if you're not quite ready to start applying. Job postings show you what kinds of experience employers are looking for in their entry-level employees, which can help you fine-tune your résumé.

RECRUITERS

Recruiters specialize in matching job seekers with jobs. They only make money when the positions are filled, so it's in their interest to hook you up with a job pronto (most recruiters are free for job seekers). Usually they take your contact info, bring you in for an interview, and then send you for another interview to publishing houses with specific needs. The flip side, though, is that some recruiters just want warm butts in seats—and they don't really care if the job's right for the person who's working at it. Here's a list of ethical recruiters who specialize in publishing.

- **Lynne Palmer Executive Recruitment,** lynnepalmerinc.com
  This highly reputable recruiting agency started out catering only to the publishing industry but now serves all areas of media and communications. Good for all positions and departments, especially editorial.

SAMPLE WANT AD

Marketing Assistant
NSR! Publishers
Duration: Full Time
Location: New York, NY
Requirements: Provides administrative and marketing support for
marketing director and others as necessary:

Duties and Responsibilities:
- Assists in all aspects of marketing, including mailings, some phases
  of planning, preparation, and follow-up for each list.
- Works with associate director of marketing on preparing meeting
  materials for marketing meetings and selling materials for our sales
  reps. Compiles and disseminates information as required.
- Types and distributes minutes from meetings; maintains mailing
  lists; assists in the preparation of sales conference and trade show
  materials.
- Routes advertising and promotional materials for approvals.
- Assists in the budgeting/forecasting process; maintains files;
  answers telephones; redirects calls; assists others in the department
  as required.
- Initiates and creates e-cards and flyers for sales reps and booksellers.
- Assists in the creation and management of back ads.

Requirements:
At least one year of relevant work experience preferred. Excellent verbal
and written communication skills. Must be detail oriented, organized,
and able to set priorities under pressure. Proficiency with Word and
Excel necessary. Familiarity with PowerPoint, FrontPage, and Outlook
helpful, but not required. Must possess college degree or equivalent work
experience.

Email: jobs@nsrpub.com
Special instructions: Please email your résumé, cover letter, and salary
requirements to Jobs@nsrpub.com with the subject line NN-MAJH. No
phone calls, please.

- **Adecco Creative,** adeccocreative.com
  A subdivision of the international recruiter Adecco, this group was founded not too long ago as a creative services provider. It caters to many markets, including publishing, advertising, and public relations. It is a great source for designers and production specialists.

- **Ribolow Associates,** ribolow.com
  This recruiting agency specializes in the publishing and advertising industries. Its sister company, Ribolow Staffing Services, also provides temporary work for publishing professionals in transition, finding them jobs in assistant editing, proofreading, copyediting, production, and graphic design among others.

Researching Specific Companies

When you're done searching publishing-specific sites and after you've registered with a recruiter (maybe), you'll want to start thinking about specific companies. Now's the time to learn everything you can about publishing's movers and shakers. Not only will your research give you a better sense of whether you'd be a good fit there, it'll also prove invaluable if and when you're lucky enough to snag an interview.

- **Print resources:** Get yourself a copy of *Jeff Herman's Guide to Book Publishers, Editors & Literary Agents* or *Literary Market Place,* and start seeing which imprints are owned by which conglomerate.

- **The company site:** Duh! Job postings can only say so much about a company, so you need to do some background research in order to really understand the books, lists, focus, and relationships among imprints. Whenever you're on a company's site, take a look at the "About Us" section. After all, the job itself (say, an editorial assistant) might seem quite appealing, but on further research, you may discover that you'd be working on books that aren't so interesting to you (golf books, perhaps, or books about Shakespeare).

  Here's another reason to go to specific company sites: Many

conglomerates don't bother posting openings to the major publishing sites, preferring only to post openings on their homepages. On that note, here's a list of URLs for the career sites for some of the biggies:

- » **Hachette Book Group,** hachettebookgroupusa.com/employment.html
- » **HarperCollins,** harpercollinscareers.com/careers
- » **Holtzbrinck Publishers,** holtzbrinckusa-jobs.com
- » **Random House,** careers.randomhouse.com
- » **Scholastic,** scholastic.com/aboutscholastic/job
- » **Simon & Schuster,** www.simonsays.com/content/consumer.cfm?app=employment&tab=1
- » **Workman,** www.workman.com/content/pagemaker.cgi?1005855037.txt
- » **W. W. Norton,** wwnorton.com/area4/jobs.htm

- **Hoover's:** This subscription site (hoovers.com)gives facts, figures, descriptions, and lists of executives for more than 43,000 companies in 600 different industries. It even lists companies' top competitors. With Hoover's, you'll always know how to answer this doozy: "Who do you think our competitors are?" Okay, so that's not a super-common question in publishing interviews, but it does come up occasionally.

- **Search engines:** If you type the name of an author, such as Jennifer Egan, you'll get 20 times as many hits as pages in her last novel. You can narrow your search by entering parts of your query in quotes, as in "Jennifer Egan" + "literary agent" or "Metropolitan Books" + "production" + "employment."

  You should also search for articles on any recent business developments in the company. If you want to impress a potential employer, show them that you're passionate about their product by being an informed consumer and job applicant. If you're applying for an assistant sales position at Loompanics and the tiny independent just got a mention in *PW*, mention it your cover letter and interview.

PUT YOUR NETWORK TO USE

Imagine going to Bloomingdale's and buying a beautiful Armani suit, bringing it home, carefully hanging it up in your closet, and then never wearing it again. Unthinkable, right? Well, you worked so hard to network back when you were preparing yourself for the job search, so why wouldn't you rely on that network now? Your list of contacts is as valuable as that Armani suit. No kidding. But like the suit, the list won't do you any good unless you use it.

66 Sometimes you might have to go through a circuitous route to arrive at your desired job. Some people work at literary agencies to network their way into a publishing house. Sometimes it's worthwhile to take a job in a department you never considered; you might find that you enjoy it—or once you gain some publishing experience, it might be easier for you to transfer to another department."

—**Julia Gilroy,** Associate Production Editor
Dutton

Reaching Out

Crack your knuckles and get ready: It's time to email everyone you've ever met in the publishing industry and then some. We're talking old bosses, fellow interns, teachers at a publishing class you took, professors from college—anyone you know who might know someone who might have access to available jobs. Start off with a simple, unobtrusive email: "Hello, I met you while I was interning at McSweeney's Books [volunteering at the Fort Greene Park Summer Festival, filing thousands of copies of *PW* at Reed, etc.], and you offered me your business card. I'm now looking for an entry-level job as a publicity assistant. Could I send you my résumé?" That's it. Don't ask them for a job; don't pester him or her for a corner office; don't list all the amazing things you've done since you last met.

As confident as you might feel in the job hunt, remember that you just started out, and you aren't entitled to a job. Be humble.

Following Up

Track the responses you get on an Excel spreadsheet so you can know at a glance who was interested, who wasn't, and whom you still need to contact. See the Career-Planning Workbook for blank forms to fill out. If somebody asks for your résumé, send it right away with a short note such as, "My résumé is attached, per your request. Please don't hesitate to pass this along to anyone who might be hiring. Thank you very much." Remember that the most successful network is one that keeps on expanding, so try to get your résumé into the hands of as many people as possible.

In the event that you don't get a reply, send a follow-up email a week later. After that, it's up to you whether you want to pursue it any further. On the one hand, emails get lost all the time, so it's possible that your two emails wound up in cyberspace somewhere. On the other hand, it's possible that the person just doesn't have the time, the interest, or—dare we say it?—the common decency to reply. Whatever you do, don't email or get in touch with the person more than three times. Just lick your wounds, cross that name off your list, and move on.

❝ I wish someone had told me how small the industry was and how each connection you make is important."

—Francine Rosado-Cruz, Human Resources Diversity Manager
Penguin Group (USA)

Building Up Your Network

Start making a conscious decision right now to seek out new people who might have job contacts or interesting insider information. Here are a few ways to add names to your list of contacts.

- **Do an internship.** Networking is yet another great reason to do an internship. But think beyond your supervisor: Your fellow interns could be the key to tipping you off about that job opening at Simon & Schuster. Introduce yourself, make friends, and get their contact info.

- **Participate in on-campus recruiting.** If you're still in college, be sure to find out which companies are visiting campus in the spring. Even if they aren't publishing related, talking to people about your interests is great networking experience. You never know how connected a human resources person in business might be. Approach reps from companies in other media and introduce yourself. Recruiters know a potentially great employee when they see one, even if that employee might not want to work for their company. Be enthusiastic about your skills and background, and listen to what they have to say. They may just lead you to the person you should be talking to.

- **Get to know the career center staff.** Make an appointment with your school's career center. Show them your résumé and seek their advice. But don't expect them to find a job for you. Come armed with questions, and use their expertise. Don't forget to send a thank-you email!

- **Contact alumni.** Your college probably has an online newsletter, bulletin board, or maybe even an alumni mentor program. Contact the alumni office or career center and ask about getting connected to alumni who work in the publishing industry.

66 I got my job through an interview I'd set up through my college's alumni network. Through that one meeting, I got two actual job interviews and eventually two job offers. When editors are looking to hire assistants, they are much more likely to listen to an editor friend's recommendation than some résumé passed to them by HR."

—**Patrick Mulligan,** Assistant Editor
Gotham Books

APPLY

Forget about landing the job for now, and definitely don't start fantasizing about having lunch at Elaine's with primo agent Andrew Wylie or kicking back a few with Akashic Books' Johnny Temple. Instead, concentrate on the more immediate goal: getting an interview. You need to get your résumé into the right hands so that you can get the right people to meet you, like you, and ultimately hire you. But to get an interview, you need to apply.

Application Tips

Now's not the time to cut corners or hand in sloppy work. Prospective employers will look over your résumé and cover letter to check your qualifications and to see whether you'd be a good fit. Go slow, and use our tips.

- **Follow the application directions exactly.** Not following directions could break your chance of getting an interview. If they want the text of your résumé in the body of an email, don't get fancy and attach a PDF or Word document—your application will likely go straight into their desktop recycling bin. Many companies ask for résumés in this format to avoid the risk of a computer virus. If they prefer that you apply using their online application, don't email or call them inquiring about a job. Apply online, just as they asked. Show companies that you know how to follow instructions by doing exactly what the job posting says.

Delete—or at the very least, clean up—your MySpace or Facebook profile. Remember: Higher-ups know how to use the Internet too.

- **Use the job posting to your advantage.** Tailor your résumé to the job posting you're applying for. This means actually mimicking the language of the job posting exactly, in either your cover letter or your résumé. If the ad says, "Office experience preferred," by all means, highlight your office experience. Ditto if the ad mentions specific computer programs such as Excel or characteristics such as "ability to multitask." Using the same language makes it easy for the employer to see that you're qualified for the job.

- **While you're sending out résumés, go ahead and send out a lot.** Send out about 20 at a time. If you can't find 20 ads to respond to, send out the rest with polite requests for informational interviews. It can't hurt. You're already *not* working there, so what's the worst that could happen? You don't get an informational interview. Big deal! Just choose another 10 companies to target.

Cover Letters

Cover letters strike fear in the hearts of even the most seasoned job seekers. After all, the cover letter determines whether your résumé gets seen or tossed in the trash. Okay, so there's a lot of pressure. But a cover letter shouldn't be a one-page summary of everything that you are, nor a clever, catchy, humorous advertisement for the perfect employee, and definitely not a sample of your creative writing. The cover letter serves the very simple but very important purpose of letting you introduce yourself to a potential employer. The cover letter should prompt the reader to turn to your résumé, then call you for an interview.

Lucky for you, there's a formula for perfect letters. Learn the formula, live the formula, and never fear cover letters again. Just to make it super-clear, we've included a sample cover letter on page 169, with numbers corresponding to each important part of the formula.

1. **Include a greeting:**
   - Always address your letter to a specific person rather than just "Dear HR" or "Good afternoon."
   - Use formal business letter format. For example, use "Dear Ms. Smith" rather than "Dear Carrie" or "Dear Carolyn." If the contact person's gender seems unclear, use "Dear Jesse Smith."

2. **State why you're writing:**
   - You're responding to an ad (from where? from when? for what?), someone (who?) recommended that you get in touch, or you're following up on (what?)

3. **Explain your current status:**
   - You're just finishing school/moving to New York/looking for an entry-level job.
   - You're available immediately/after you graduate/next fall (for an internship).

4. **List your assets:**
   - Tell what sets you apart. (In other words, give a sense of why they should hire you.) Offer a recap of your major publishing-related accomplishments/awards/studies. Yes, they'll see how great you are once they check out your résumé—think of the cover letter as your chance to give a little taste before the main meal. Don't forget to target this list toward the job posting.
   - Demonstrate your knowledge of publishing, especially the books the company publishes.

5. **Discuss why you want to work there:**
   - Explain what is it about the company or its books that makes you want to work there.

6. **Reiterate the "fit":**
   - Make the case for why they should hire you. Remember, it's not just about what the company can do for you but also about what you can do for them. Tie in your assets and your attraction to the company. Sell yourself!

SAMPLE COVER LETTER

Raul Garcia
1112 Carpenter St.
Charlottesville, VA 22111

Patrick Gross
Scholastic Inc.
557 Broadway
New York, NY 10012

March 9, 2007

(1) — Dear Mr. Gross:

(2) — I was thrilled to see your ad posted yesterday on the *Publishers Weekly* job
board for a hardcover design assistant. I've just received a bachelor's in graphic — (3)
design from the Rhode Island School of Design, and I am looking for entry-
level job in book design. My résumé is attached.

(4) — As a student, I've had classes in typography, color theory, InDesign, QuarkX-
Press, Photoshop, and Illustrator. I have a passion for books, especially
children's books, and have worked throughout the school year at a children's
bookstore near my college. I've spent the past three summers as a youth
camp counselor, so I have a great familiarity and understanding of children's
interests and needs. I'm now ready to begin a career in book publishing,
preferably as a designer of children's books.

(5) — Scholastic has been quite a presence in my life since childhood—I used to
read *Highlights* magazine religiously and order from the Scholastic Book Club
catalogs. Even now, I've read all the Harry Potter books! The challenge of — (6)
designing books for such an impressionable audience—children—is very
exciting to me, and I'm eager to pursue the first steps in my career. I am confident that my technical skills and experience with children would benefit
your company.

(7) — I can be reached by email at rgarcia@professionalemail.com or by cell phone
at (703) 555-2210. Thank you in advance for your time and consideration. I
hope to hear from you soon.

Sincerely,

Raul Garcia

7. **Give your contact info:**
   - Let them know the best way to reach you. Provide your landline and cell phone numbers, as well as the (professional!) email address you're using for your job search.

INTERVIEW

You came, you saw, you applied—and you landed your first interview. Congratulations! Go out and celebrate. When you're finished celebrating, continue reading below . . .

❝ Always be considerate to everyone you come across as you're looking for a job: the assistant who answers the phone, the fellow underling waiting for an interview in the lobby, the random employee in a department you don't understand. All these people might pop up again over the course of your publishing career, and it will behoove you to have been kind to them the first time around. I'm not saying you have to kiss up to people; just be courteous. That person who seems annoying—or irrelevant—might be a colleague someday."

—Erin Edmison, Literary Scout
Mary Anne Thompson Associates

The interview is your chance to convince an employer that you're the perfect person for the job. To some extent, the interview matters more than your cover letter and résumé combined, but don't let this fact scare you. (Easy for us to say, we know.) But seriously, the emphasis placed on the interview is a good thing. No longer are you depending on just a piece of paper or two to sell you to an employer. Now you can do the selling yourself. Calm your nerves by preparing for the interview. Be ready, professional, and impressive, and you'll be good to go.

Nailing the Interview

Being prepared for your interview involves a little bit of background research combined with a lot of common sense, politeness, and composure. Before you head to the office, all dolled up in your suit, make sure you do the following.

- **Know about the company and job you're applying for.** Know what books they publish and what types of books you'd be working on. Also, make sure you've read up about the company—if they've just been sold, for example, or how many bestsellers they have on the *New York Times* list.

- **Know what you can offer them, not what they can offer you.** Remember they're looking for someone who, with his or her skills and talent, can improve the company in some way. Be ready to discuss exactly what assets you bring to the company, whether it's three years as a graphic designer, a solid background in grammar, a thorough knowledge of the symbols used by proofreaders, or a genuine love of books.

- **Dress nicely.** Your appearance could have a greater effect than you'd like, so think about what you are wearing. Make sure your outfit is ironed and free of rips or holes. Take out your piercings; cover your tats. Refrain from wearing heavy makeup, loud jewelry, or strong perfume. In short, don't wear anything that might district the interviewer. You don't have to go corporate, but you should look like a young professional.

- **Show up 10 minutes early.** That way, if you're nervous, you can get a drink of water, fix your hair, or practice deep breathing before you head inside. Hey, an interview's like a deadline—show employers that you can meet deadlines by being early or on time.

- **Make eye contact and shake hands.** But don't make the interviewer feel uncomfortable by staring or by giving a Vulcan death grip. Look away occasionally or try looking at the person's forehead sometimes. As for the handshake, shake like you mean it, not like you want to break the interviewer's hand off. On the flip side, don't give a limp-fish handshake, either.

- **Sit up straight.** Don't slouch. Don't lean too far forward, because that can make you seem juvenile and too eager. But don't lean too far back, since that can make you seem like you don't care. And always keep your hands in your lap.

- **Ask for water.** If you're offered a beverage, keep it simple. It won't surprise you, won't be too hot, and won't make you jittery. And you'll have some on hand in case you get a dry mouth or cough (which happens a lot during interviews).

- **Limit each of your answers to less than two minutes.** Believe it or not, interviewers prefer that you talk less and listen more. Your ability to be concise will be noticed.

- **Eradicate *like*, *you know*, *huh*, and other slang words from your speech.** Be articulate, be eloquent, and be polite.

- **Storytell.** The best way to show who you are is to accompany your answers with stories and details. If you tell them you're a self-starter, describe an experience in which you started yourself. It's not enough to say, "I know how to manage my time." Tell a story in which you managed a part-time job, a sick cat, and six finals. These examples can also make you stand out as a candidate, since anyone can name the same traits.

SPARK YOUR CAREER IN BOOK PUBLISHING

Interview Dos and Don'ts

DON'T

... Chew gum during the interview
... Have a cigarette beforehand
... Wear heavy perfume, cologne, or makeup
... Come in with a list of all the things you categorically refuse to do on the job
... Put down anyone (like a current boss or teacher) or any other company
... Crack any jokes that your interviewer might find offensive

DO

... Turn off your cell phone
... Sit up straight and avoid slouching
... Show that you're listening attentively by nodding or saying "Right" or "I see" when appropriate
... Dress up a little rather than down a little
... Smile—with your eyes, if possible

Typical Interview Queries

Be ready to respond to the following statements and questions.

- ***Tell me about yourself.*** This is not a request for an oral autobiography, so don't start with your favorite movie or why your parents named you Sunshine (although we'd be interested in hearing more about that . . .). Instead, briefly summarize what you've been doing in college or since college—*briefly* being the operative word.

- ***Why do you want to go into the publishing industry?*** Start with what you like about the publishing industry and what you like about this particular company. An easy answer is, "I love books," so don't just say that. This may be the reason, but expand on it. What exactly do you love about them and why? How would you like to participate in creating or marketing or selling them? When did you first realize that publishing was for you?

- **Why do you want to work for us?** You might like their books, the authors they publish, or the editors they employ. Be ready to explain why you're enthusiastic about their books or imprint personality and what you can bring to the job.

- **What are your favorite books?/Tell me about the last book you read./What book is currently on your nightstand?** You pretty much can't avoid being asked one of these questions. Be prepared to answer it honestly and thoroughly.

66 My job interview with my last boss consisted of talking about *Infinite Jest* for 20 minutes. Editors want to see that you're passionate about books and that you're widely read. You should also have a familiarity with *The New Yorker*, *The Atlantic*, and *Harper's*."

—**Patrick Mulligan,** Assistant Editor
Gotham Books

- **What are your strengths?** Don't be modest. This is your chance to shine. Remember to give examples of how you've exhibited these strengths. If you're an exceptional leader, discuss how you decided to reorganize the volunteers at 826New York or led your tennis team to the state finals while making everyone bond over *The Rivals* (which discusses the rivalry between Chris Evert and Martina Navratilova).

- **What are your weaknesses?** Employers know you're human, but they want to make sure that you know you're human. It's okay to be confident, but don't be so confident that you don't have an answer to this question. You're just starting out, so you have a lot to learn about the industry. Make your weaknesses sound positive by explaining what you've learned from them or how you've worked to transform them into strengths. Try to turn them into strengths. For example, if you're a perfectionist, say that you want everything to be perfect because you take great pride in your work.

- **Tell me about your work experience.** This is when you can talk about how much you learned at that summer internship answering phones at Arcade Publishing or about your part-time job at the library in order to show your prospective employer how willing you are to learn. This is your chance to explain how what you've done relates to the job you're interviewing for.

66 Make sure to have a running list of your favorite books/authors stashed away in your brain, because guaranteed someone will ask you about them and you'll completely forget all their names. It happened to me."

—**Corinne Kalasky,** Assistant Publicist
HarperCollins Publishers

- **Do you have questions for me?** The interview isn't just about the company interviewing you—it's also your chance to interview the company. After all, the company needs to be a right fit for you. Plus, you'll make a much better impression if you show interest in their company and their books by demonstrating that you're looking for more than just a way to pay the bills.

At the end of the interview, your interviewer will probably ask if you have any questions. Don't screw things up by saying, "No, thanks." Instead, ask any or all of the following:

  » *What are you looking for in an employee?*
  » *What's your management style?*
  » *What are your favorites among the books you work on?*
  » *What do you like about this company?*
  » *How did you end up where you are in publishing?*
  » *What's a typical day like for you?*
  » *What are the responsibilities that the job entails?*
  » *What benefits does the company offer?*
  » *How would you describe the imprint's "personality"?*
  » *Is there room for employee advancement?*

66 We're not a nation of book-buying, book-loving folks, and publishers are for-profit companies, so be prepared to be a creative editor, a bottom-line thinker, a marketing maven, a public advocate, and an all-around cheerleader to champion the book projects you love."

—**Sheila Keenan,** Executive Editor
Scholastic

After the Interview

After the interview, you've still got some work to do (sorry). Send a unique thank-you to each and every person who interviewed you. Email is fine, as long as you keep it professional and as long as you don't send an email blast to all three people you met. They took the time to talk to you, so take the time to thank them individually. If you don't do email, type your thank-you. Just don't handwrite something: Rather than charming, interviewers might see a handwritten note as anachronistic.

Your thank-you note should not only thank the interviewer but also mention a few specific things learned during the interview and remind the interviewer of why you're right for the job. Most important, you should concisely come off as grateful and specific. There's no need to send flowers or a fruit basket. No, really—just send a thank-you.

Second and Third Interviews

The usual interview drill goes something like this: first interview with someone in human resources, second interview with the person who'll be managing you, and third interview with either the person who'll be managing you and/or her boss. Think of it this way:

- HR makes sure you're not a psycho.
- The prospective boss makes sure you're an okay person who's got the skills for the job.
- The boss's boss makes sure you're not a psycho (again).

The first interview gives you a chance to get some general info about the job and company, while the second and third interview give you a chance to ask specific, targeted questions about your day-to-day responsibilities. The later interviews also give you a chance to get to know the people for and with whom you'd actually be working.

SAMPLE THANK-YOU NOTE

Dear Ms. Schwartz:

Thank you for taking the time to talk with me yesterday afternoon about working at Carroll & Graf. I have always been inspired by the books your house publishes, and now I see why.

Specifically, I enjoyed seeing the shelves filled with the books from your most recent summer list and glancing at cover designs for the next list. After our talk, I am even more excited about an opportunity to work in your managing editorial department. I can be reached by phone (555.811.5555) or email (k.peacock@college.edu).

Sincerely,

Katie Peacock

Katie Peacock

66 Don't be discouraged if no one calls regarding an open position. Some positions can take months to fill. I applied for a job in May and heard from the company in late August. A friend applied for a job in the fall and didn't start until the end of January. Also, don't always assume that you're a horrible candidate if you don't hear back from companies. Many decide to fill positions in-house, so don't always assume it's 'you' who isn't qualified."

—**Lindsay Weiskittel,** Editorial Assistant
SparkNotes

Making a Decision

Spend some time after the interview reviewing your notes (you did take notes, yes?). Carefully consider whether the job's right for you even before you find out about whether you got a second interview. Wait until you get all offers in to decide which job you'd like to take.

If you get offered a great job but have already accepted another, think carefully before you bail. It's a small world out there, and you can spoil your reputation if you handle the situation poorly. When weighing options, consider the following.

- **What will you be doing all day?** If the daily tasks themselves don't interest you, you'll need some other motivation for working there, whether it's the potential for advancement or the prestige of the company.

- **Who's on your team?** Your coworkers and your boss make a huge difference in your work world.

- **What do they make?** No, we're not talking about dollars; we're talking about types of books. If you can't get excited about the company's books, it'll be much harder to get excited about actually working on them.

- **Where is it?** Location matters. If your family needs you in Missouri, it could be hard to take a job in New York—or vice versa.

- **What next?** In a small company, you might rise quickly to the top (while still doing all your own paperwork, faxing, and filing). In a large company, there may be more opportunities for advancement, but it'll probably take you longer to reach your ideal position.

- **What comes with the deal?** Benefits, including health care, paid vacation, profit sharing, and employee discounts, often cost the company up to 30 percent of your salary. Some companies might pay you less but offer you more, such as four weeks of vacation or paid dental and vision insurance. Look at the total package, and don't just focus on salary.

- **Is the money comparable?** Notice that we list money last. We know it's important, but if the money is comparable, think carefully about the other parts of the offer. And if the money isn't comparable, you should still be thinking about the other parts of the job first! Life's too short to do something you're not excited about, with people you don't get along with, in a company whose products make you yawn uncontrollably even if you're being paid muchos dólares to work there.

66 If you're offered a job that scares you because it seems like a 'big' job, take it. Never take a job because you think, 'Well, I can do that—it won't be that hard.' You'll be bored out of your mind in two months. Always go for the challenge."

—**Andrea Colvin,** Executive Managing Editor
Harry N. Abrams

SAYING *NO* GRACIOUSLY

If you do need to turn a job down, don't burn your bridges. Be polite and gracious, and thank your contact for his or her time and attention. Remember, everyone you meet in the industry has the potential to be a future colleague (or boss). And remember, part two: Don't feel bad if you have to turn down a job. After all, your first priority is to find a match that works for you *and* the company, not just the company.

7

NAVIGATING YOUR FIRST JOB

We're not gonna lie to you: Navigating your first job will be tough. Not only will you have to adjust to getting up early in the morning and wearing something other than sweats and flip-flops all day but you'll also have to learn how to please your boss, manage your workload, and be a publishing professional. Plus, you'll need to start thinking long term, specifically about where you'd like to be career-wise in the next few years. Trust us 'cause we've been there: It's a lot to handle. But not to worry. This chapter shows you how to survive—and thrive—in your first job.

BRUSH UP ON WORK BEHAVIOR 101

As the Beastie Boys once sang, you need "skills to pay the bills." Since you got the job, we know you've got the publishing skills. But do you have the office skills? We're not talking about knowing how to work the coffee machine either. How you behave at work is as important as how well you perform your duties. In other words, professionalism counts. To move ahead in publishing, you need to be a master of office politics, a true team player, and more. Make common courtesy and common sense your constant guides.

10 Ways to Get Yourself Fired (Or At Least Not Promoted) From Your First Job

Don't believe us? Try one of the following behaviors at work—and don't say we didn't warn you.

1. Dress yourself straight out of Hot Topic. (Keep your cleavage and your thighs covered. This goes double for you, gentlemen.)

2. Say "no" a lot, especially to your boss.

3. Gossip.

4. Date anyone at the office. Better yet, date your boss.

5. Spend your day IM'ing or gabbing on your cell phone.

6. Take off at 5 P.M. every day.

7. Go behind your supervisor's back.

8. Tip your friends and family off to "insider secrets."

9. Give out manuscripts or ARCs without permission.

10. Cry, yell, or throw things.

The Basic Rules

Whether you're at the powerful Wylie Agency or tiny Mountaineers Books, the art department or in sales, the same rules of office behavior apply. Break them at your own risk.

- **Be there.** This simple command means a whole lot of things. Be there every day. Be there on time. Be there getting things done (not just browsing). Be there during meetings. Just because your boss can't see you doodling doesn't mean someone else can't—and this person could be as critical to your career as your boss (this person could be your boss's close friend and office confidante, or she could be your boss's boss). You're not in nursery school anymore, so leave the childish behavior at home.

- **Be careful about what you say and type.** You never know who might be coming around the corner, so keep the "Whoa, mama, didn't she wear that skirt yesterday?" comments to yourself. Embrace the "inner" part of your inner monologue, and don't make snide remarks about your coworkers. Same goes for email: Anything you write can be forwarded without your knowledge to someone else, like your supervisor. If you wouldn't say it out loud, don't put it in an email, even if you use a nonwork account, such as Gmail or Yahoo. Think before you send. Most companies monitor their employees' email and Internet activity anyway, so refrain from cursing or gossiping on company time.

❝ I got an email from my boss that I thought was totally ridiculous—so ridiculous a little voice inside my head told me to forward it to a coworker. How could I know that my boss would arrive at my coworker's desk at the same moment as my 'isn't this the dumbest thing you've ever seen' email popped up on the computer screen? I didn't get fired, thank goodness, but I did get a stern talking-to about professional behavior."

—An anonymous editor

- **Be helpful.** Think fast: A marketing manager comes up to your desk and asks you to help him sort envelopes for a mailing to *Bookforum*. Trouble is, you don't work in the marketing department. Do you (a) turn up your nose and go back to filing your nails or (b) pitch in and help out? The answer, we hope, is obvious. You should always be willing to help out, regardless of how menial the job is or who's asking you to do the work.

- **Be neat.** Chances are, your mom doesn't work in your office, so don't expect someone to clean up after you. Keep your work area spick-and-span. Before you leave for the day, put away any loose papers. Buy some dusting wipes and use them. Don't keep perishable food (such as fruit) in your desk. A messy desk doesn't make you look creative—it makes you look sloppy.

- **Be discreet.** Everybody has a personal life, even that boring guy who works in payroll and makes rubber-band balls in between cutting checks. But your coworkers don't need to know about your roommate's stinky foot disease or your late-night Internet chat "dates." When you start making friends, you can talk about your other interests over lunch or after work. When you're on the clock, though, keep your personal life personal.

- **Be respectful of your coworkers.** Just as you should keep your personal life personal, so you should respect others' personal lives. Don't invade their privacy or personal space. Remember, hearing someone on the phone discussing her kid's behavioral problems or negotiating with an agent doesn't give you license to ask personal questions once she hangs up. Also, show consideration for your colleagues by recognizing their experience in the industry and asking for their opinions. You can learn a lot from these people, so develop good working relationships with them.

- **Be friendly.** A smile goes a long way. Publishing is a small world, and what goes around definitely comes around. So say "hello," "please," "thank you," and "have a great weekend." Make an effort to get to know everyone's name, what they do, and a little tidbit about them such as their birthday or favorite book. Make another effort to remember all that info about everyone in your office. As a young professional, you're part of a team, so get to know your teammates.

- **Be patient.** Maybe you think you and Nicole Aragi have so much in common that you should be BFF, or maybe you think Sonny Mehta should be coming to you for advice. But the truth is that you're going to have to become BFF with the fax machine before you get even kinda close to taking a lunch with an agent or hanging out with a CEO. Publishing's an apprenticeship business: You start at the ground floor, and you work yourself up.

Think before you blog

Sure, some people blog about work and get away with it. And some people blog about work, get fired, and then land a huge book deal for a thinly veiled roman à clef. But the truth is that blogging about work is a bad, bad idea. Never underestimate your coworkers' sleuthing capabilities: No matter how clever you think you are, eventually someone you work with will discover your blog. And the results won't be pretty. Even if you don't get fired (and yes, that's a big if), you'll probably get frozen out of good projects and promotions. Nobody likes a tattletale, especially an anonymous electronic one. Don't blog at work, and don't blog about work.

MANAGE YOUR OFFICE RELATIONSHIPS

It's a sad fact of the working world that you'll often spend more time with your coworkers than with your loved ones or friends. Sadder still is the fact that you'll spend as much time at work scoping the scene and navigating office politics as you will, well, working. The trick to maintaining a good working environment is simple: Always be polite and professional when dealing with coworkers.

You and Your Boss

The word *boss* strikes fear in the hearts of most employees, especially young people and publishing professionals who aren't fans of Bruce Springsteen. Before you cower under your desk and refuse to come out at the sound of the b-word, remember that your relationship with your first boss will likely be one of the most significant relationships of your whole career. Good or bad, draconian or buddy-buddy, your first boss will be your first teacher in publishing. You'll learn a lot from him or her, no matter what.

Your primary responsibility in an entry-level job will be helping your boss meet his or her objectives. Whether it's sending out manuscripts, answering phones and taking messages, or updating schedules and databases, everything you do goes toward making your boss look good. Your boss counts on you to help ensure that things run smoothly. Proving that you can be a competent assistant is the first step toward acquiring responsibilities, authority, and, someday, an assistant of your own.

66 My first boss made me book all of her appointments, including scheduling her gynecological exams."

—A former agent's assistant

Pretend you're an anthropologist and observe your boss as you would a unique creature from another culture. What time does she come in? Does she eat at her desk a lot? Does she prefer email or face-to-face communication? How often does she call in sick, leave early, raise her voice, or dole out praise? Is she a fan of paper clips or binder clips? We're not recommending you go all *Single White Female*, but merely that you observe your boss to discover her likes and dislikes. Getting to know your boss's work style will go a long way toward facilitating a strong working relationship. After a while, you'll probably fall into a groove with your boss in which you can anticipate what she wants and how she wants it. Until then, keep these tips in mind.

- **Communicate like your boss.** Does she like formal memos or quick email updates? Should you always include a cover letter with any work you give her to review? Some bosses like a daily status report, some prefer a weekly check in, and some want you to do your own thing without bothering them—ever. Some bosses like to call you, even if you sit just a few feet away, and some will rely exclusively on email. Take mental notes about how your boss likes her information and shift your own communication style accordingly.

- **Ask questions.** If you don't understand, ask. It's far better to ask for clarification than to forge ahead incorrectly and make costly mistakes. Make sure you always know exactly what you need to do on any given assignment by getting answers to specific questions. Instead of saying, "I don't know how to do this" (which obviously isn't really a question), say, "How do we determine the Canadian prices for each possible U.S. price of a book?" or, "Who would I talk to in the legal department about obtaining permission for this song lyric?" or, "On what day and at what time do the production status meetings take place?"

- **Double- and triple-check your work.** Your boss doesn't have time to give you endless feedback or opportunities for revision. Always review and edit your work carefully. Double- and triple-check it for mistakes. Publishing, after all, is about the craft of words, so any work you do in-house, whether a short email or a long proposal about a new series, should be error-free. And remember, presentation counts. Check that whatever you give your boss—flap copy, manuscripts, spreadsheets, copies, etc.—is neat and in order.

- **Never correct your boss during a meeting.** Even if he's wrong, don't embarrass him in front of his colleagues and employees. Stop at his office or send him an email with the correct information after the meeting. Make sure you tell him how you know that he made a mistake. Don't say, "You were wrong. Ha!" Instead, say something like,

"Having run the ARCs over to marketing this morning, I know that the new Grisham title is pubbing in October, not July." Then offer to help him rectify the mistake if possible: "Would you like me to send around an email with the new pub date?"

Bosses are people too

It's easy to deify—or vilify—your boss. Before you imagine your boss as a god or a devil, remember that your boss is human and as error-prone as everyone else. Bosses make mistakes, lose their tempers, fight with their spouses or friends, wake up on the wrong side of the bed, and get overworked and overwhelmed. When you think your boss is acting unfairly toward you, stop and think. What could be motivating her behavior? Have I seen her act like this before? If so, when? What can I do to make the situation better for her? A simple, "Are you okay?" or, "Is there anything I can do?" goes a long way toward reminding your boss that she might be acting like a psycho. When things go wrong and your boss is upset, think about her goals, motivation, and position in the current situation and you'll be less likely to take things as personally.

That said, if your boss treats you poorly for fun, get thee to human resources. Run, don't walk, to HR if your boss ever abuses you verbally or physically or if your boss asks you to:

- Not file taxes or fill out tax forms
- Lie
- Delete emails or shred important papers
- Doctor contracts or documents
- Babysit his or her kids
- Go out on a date with someone he or she recommends
- Spy or report on coworkers
- Spend your own money without being reimbursed
- Hang out one-on-one outside of work
- Perform sexual favors

No amount of sensitivity on your part can make a truly bad, pathological boss who treats you like crap all the time become better.

- **Make your boss look good.** If your boss is on the way to a meeting and you know he should have the manuscript/production status report/flap copy/cover design specs, politely stop him before he walks into the conference room. Ask him if he has everything he needs. If he says "yes," ask a more direct question, such as, "Do you have the most recent publication schedule?" You'll also want to remind your boss of the interesting tidbits you've learned about your coworkers, without sounding like a creep: "Did you know that the art director's birthday is next week? Would you like me to order some cupcakes?" People in publishing love cupcakes. Seriously.

- **When you don't know something, admit it.** Usually a simple, "I don't know," will do. Whenever you can, follow up that admission with a precise offer to find out the info, such as, "Let me double-check the print run and let you know ASAP," or, "I expect the author's comments on the page proofs to be here by Thursday." If you have enough information to make an educated guess, do so, but don't fake it if you don't have a clue. Your ignorance—and unwillingness to admit your lack of knowledge—will only get you into trouble later.

- **Make *yes* your favorite word.** Deadlines matter in publishing. A lot. But people get behind all the time, so your boss might ask you to pitch in somewhere else in the company. If she asks you to do something, do it willingly while being clear about your other responsibilities. Say something like, "I'd be happy to help publicity sort those dummies. The only catch is I'll have to put off updating the status report until later this week. Is that okay with you?"

DEALING WITH AN OLDER BOSS

A lot of recent college grads have a specific set of expectations about their careers and work environments. They think it's okay to speak their minds, regardless of circumstances, and they assume that their opinions will be highly valued and, more important, followed. They expect immediate gratification and a fast climb up the corporate ladder.

Hey, we hear you. We understand that you're self-confident and self-motivated. And that's why you were hired. Still, you need to be respectful of the job culture in your office, especially of the Generation X-ers and baby boomers who'll probably be your bosses. Those folks often consider recent grads to be impatient whiners who think they're entitled to everything the world has to offer. Don't give your older bosses the opportunity to believe that stereotype. Be humble and be patient.

Okay, so maybe your boss has been in publishing since books were printed on papyrus. Maybe he doesn't get how to attach documents to email—and maybe the only Sidekick he knows is Batman's good buddy Robin. Ignore the temptation to make fun of him. Instead, think of his age as an asset: It means he knows a whole lot about the biz. He's been around the block a few times, and he'd probably relish the opportunity to show a young whippersnapper like you a few old-school tricks. Ask questions. Be respectful and professional. Hopefully, though, he won't call you a "whippersnapper."

❝ So I filled in for the assistant to the VP of publishing. The VP, who'd clearly been loafing in the upper echelon of book publishing for decades, bungled his way through the morning, deleting important emails, and tearing his hair out while searching for a manuscript from a big-deal agent. Lunch arrived, and the VP turned to me, distressed: 'They forgot the forks! Where am I going to get a fork?!' The kitchen nook across the hall was apparently too far a journey for him, so when I returned with a hand-ful of plastic utensils in hand, he was amazed at my resourcefulness. 'They have forks in the kitchen? How smart!' Smart, indeed."

—A former editorial assistant

DEALING WITH A YOUNGER BOSS

Having a younger boss can be amazing. She'll understand you, because she'll share your pop culture references. At the very least, she'll under-stand how to work a computer. You'll have a lot in common with each other, so you'll probably find it easier to communicate with her. The chal-lenge: It's easy to think of your boss as your friend, forgetting that she's your supervisor. You may love the idea of working with a cool boss with whom you could hit the sample sales or kick back a few after work. But all friendships can go sour, and the last thing you want is a boss who's miffed that you didn't show up last weekend to help her move into her new apartment.

Even if you and your boss share a birthday, you can't ever forget that she's in charge. As such, your younger boss should always be treated with as much respect as you'd accord someone much older than you. Don't go into excessive detail about your private life; don't share stories about drunken nights, walks of shame, bad roommates, or drug use. You can't assume that private confessions will stay private, so save the gory stories for your pals.

Sometimes you'll find that your boss might be the one crossing the line. She might see you as a younger sibling and thus want to impress you with her hip, happenin' life. Combat a boss who overshares by nodding politely, chuckling at the appropriate moments, and smiling a lot. Ignore the temptation to try to outdo her with a, "Hey, if you think that was bad, let me tell you about the time . . ."

66 My first boss was only three years older than I was. At first, it was fun: We liked the same music, and we took smoke breaks together. But eventually she started blurring the boundaries, such as the time she asked me to file some papers while she went into X-rated detail about her sex life. Needless to say, I decided to find a new job, one with a boss who would teach me about publishing—not about blow jobs."

—An anonymous production editor

Staff Hierarchies and Office Politics

Every office has office politics, regardless of whether you work in a gigantic office with thousands of employees or a three-person house. Be careful, and tread lightly at first. Get to know who holds the official power (such as the publisher or editor in chief) and who holds the unofficial power (a favorite senior editor or a treasured graphic artist). While you might want to jump in and make friends by sharing your life story, be discreet and cautious about what you say to whom when. This discretion and caution will definitely pay off later on.

Here are some other guidelines for dealing with office politics.

- **Know the hierarchy.** You'll quickly learn who wields the power around your office. Still, respect everyone, even those people low on the power totem pole. If an assistant editor who's been there a year longer than you makes a suggestion, listen to her. Be respectful of her seniority. Listen to her opinions and understand that you can learn from everyone at the company, not only your boss.

- **Shut out the office soap opera.** People complain about their coworkers—it's a fact of life. Do your best to stay neutral. Saying something like, "Maybe I'm not the best person to hear this," to evade a potentially uncomfortable (and unwise) discussion is totally fine. What you absolutely don't want to do is turn around and repeat what you've heard to your office friends. Gossip spreads fast, and long after everyone's forgotten the time the managing editor dressed down a production editor in a meeting, people will remember that you told everyone you knew about what you saw and heard. A reputation for being indiscreet will definitely hurt your chances for promotion down the road.

- **Dot your *i*'s, cross your *t*'s, and keep your mouth shut.** Do your work well, do your work thoroughly, and do your work on time. Figure out how to stay organized, whether by using an online calendar or through an old-fashioned day planner. If you're unsure about whether you're doing a project correctly, ask your boss for some quick feedback. Don't complain about your workload. It's the twenty-first century, and everyone's busy. Nobody wants to hear about how boring or taxing your entry-level job is.

- **Remember, life's not fair.** Sometimes it might seem as if your boss only shows the love to a few people in your department. Try not to obsess about whom she favors. Remember that everyone has to start somewhere, and concentrate on contributing to the greater goal of producing solid, saleable books. If, after a while, you don't feel as if your work has been recognized, find an appropriate way to share your accomplishments with your boss. Let her know what a great job you've been doing through a status report or a quick meeting.

- **Don't expect a "thank-you."** Yes, everybody likes to be thanked, and everybody likes praise. But the fact is that a lot of professionals don't "see" assistants. The people who make the coffee, update the databases, and distribute the mail simply don't exist for some publishing professionals. Don't take it personally. Do your job competently and completely, say "yes" a lot, and eventually you'll get noticed.

- **Get a rep for being a team player.** As you toil away at the entry level, develop a good work attitude. Smile and say "yes" a lot. When you finish a project, for example, ask for something else to do. When you see a coworker struggling to fix a paper jam in the copier, offer to help out. When you're heading out for coffee, ask if you can bring something back for your cubemates. Get in early and stay late. Your enthusiasm and thoughtfulness will be remembered.

- **Leave your ego at home.** Remember how annoying it was back in college when people would brag about their SAT scores or replay high school highlights? Work's exactly like college in that respect: Nobody cares what you did before you got your job. Obviously you must have done something well, because you're there working, so there's no need to regale your coworkers with the time you scored 15 goals in that field hockey game or hang up your diploma from Fancy Pants U. Sure, you have a right to be proud of your accomplishments, but the fact is that your coworkers only care about whether you do your job well.

Mixing Business with Pleasure

Scary but true: As a full-time employee, you'll spend around 120,000 minutes at work each year. So, of course, you're going to want to make friends with the people sitting next to you for 40 hours a week, 50 weeks a year. And you should, because work friends are great. They'll keep you from stabbing yourself with paper clips when things get crazy at the office. Unlike your family or other friends, work friends always understand what you're going through when reviewing blues or checking corrections.

Work relationships, though, are a special breed of friendship and should be treated accordingly. After all, the nice coworker with whom you're sharing lunches every Tuesday could suddenly become your superior after the next annual review. Another tricky situation occurs when you and your good office pal are competing for the same promotion. We've said it before, and we'll say it again: You can't go wrong by avoiding gossip and by keeping your work life separate from your personal life.

66 From stapler stealing to cubicle hovering, an old design colleague of mine had no idea about boundaries. If she had computer trouble, she'd practically wheel me away from my desk and continue working from my computer. One morning, she couldn't get her Mac to work. She spent 10 minutes banging the mouse on her desktop. After a bathroom run, I returned to my computer to find my mouse missing and my InDesign frozen. I spent the next hour thanking my lucky stars that I'm an obsessive document saver."

—An anonymous graphic designer

SOCIALIZING WITH COWORKERS

Socializing with your coworkers is definitely a do. Work won't be too fun if you don't have any friends, so make an effort to talk to the people around you. Ask them about their weekends, and tell them about a great movie or band you saw. Let them know when Malcolm Gladwell, Jonathan Lethem, or some other brand-name author's giving a reading. You're there to work, obviously, but you're also a part of a team—and nobody likes a grouch. Nobody likes a clique either, so be careful about only chatting with certain people.

Nurture your work relationships by going out for happy hour, participating in company-sponsored events, and asking people to have lunch once in a while. Think of it as networking: You never know where your officemate might be in five years. Try to talk with everybody in your department on a regular basis. Tell stories, relax, and have a good time, within reason. Anything you do or say to your coworkers in the off-hours shouldn't be something that you wouldn't do or say to them during the workday.

DATING AT WORK

Once you've made some friends at work, you might decide to start making a few "more than friends." Think really, really hard before you date your coworkers. Dating can be complicated under the best of circumstances, but dating at work presents a whole new set of challenges. What if you get assigned to work on a project together? Can you maintain professional distance even after you've seen each other naked? Can you go from having a big fight with your honey the night before to exchanging office pleasantries the next morning? And what if you break up? You and your coworker will have to answer these and lots of other awkward questions. Before you date at work, ask yourself this one: Is it worth it?

Some companies have policies that prohibit colleagues from dating one another, and just about all companies prohibit bosses from dating their employees. But love is blind, as they say, and so true love—and lust—transcends cubicle walls. If you fall in love or into bed with a coworker, whatever you do, keep your romance out of the office. We mean it: Seal those lips from 9 to 5. Don't broadcast details at the water cooler the next day. Likewise, kissing near the supplies closet might seem like a romantic notion, but nobody wants to see or hear you being naughty. Always treat each other formally and professionally, even if you call each other "Snoopy" and "Poopy" outside of the office.

10 Things to Avoid at the Company Holiday Party

1. Only hanging out with your team. You see these people all day, every day. Use the office party as an opportunity to see what the guy in the cube next door does.

2. Making fun of your coworkers. Always a no-no, regardless of how drunk the intern gets or how ugly your boss's suit is.

3. Getting trashed. Think dignity. Don't think par-tay!

4. Dressing or dancing inappropriately. Save the tube tops and grinding for Saturday night.

5. Adding a little sumthin'-sumthin' to the punch bowl.

6. Bringing manuscripts for your boss to look at.

7. Making out with your date by the bathrooms all night.

8. Making out with your coworkers anywhere.

9. Letting a boss or coworker know how you really feel.

10. Arm wrestling, body slamming, or fighting.

TAKE CRITICISM GRACEFULLY

It's funny how everybody's a critic, yet nobody likes to be criticized. None-theless, giving and receiving feedback happens to be a major part of life at work. If you've been a student until now, you might be used to a certain type of feedback—and you might see your boss as another professor. Don't. Your boss isn't there to give you an A, so you need to readjust your expectations. As a new employee, you'll inevitably screw up. Accept that now, and you'll be much happier down the road. Remember that even the mega-powerful publisher Steve Rubin had to start somewhere.

Even if you manage to steer clear of major catastrophes, your supervisors will still point out ways you could improve your work, behavior, sense of organization, and so on. Trust us: There will always be *something* you could be doing better, faster, more efficiently. Being told that you need to improve something isn't the end of the world. After all, to err is human, as the saying goes.

See criticism as a chance to learn something new. When your boss tells you that you should never, ever keep Jane Friedman or Sessalee Hensley on hold, listen carefully to what he says. If you don't understand why these women can't wait like everyone else, politely ask for clarification. Above all, don't cry! Suck it up. Then take notes and really focus on doing it better next time. Neither you nor your boss wants to have this conversation again. It's awkward for your boss too.

During the conversation with your supervisor, own your mistakes and accept responsibility for what you did incorrectly. Don't make excuses; don't talk about what you did right or well. Again, listen to your boss, then simply apologize. A heartfelt, "I'm sorry, and it won't happen again," will not only show your boss that you take your job seriously but will also demonstrate your maturity. Whereas children whine and cry when criticized, adults accept criticism gracefully, understand the errors they made, and move on. Promise your boss that you'll do better next time—and follow through on that promise.

Dealing with the Dreaded Annual Review

If you've got a job, you'll eventually get an annual review. The truth is, nobody likes annual reviews, and, honestly, probably nobody will ever read your annual review once your boss files it with human resources. Most of the time, the paperwork gets stuck in a filing cabinet, never to see the light of day again (unless your boss wants to fire you, in which case your reviews will get closely examined for patterns of bad behavior). Nevertheless, at some point during your first job, your boss will want to have a sit-down chat with you about your overall performance.

Rather than freaking out, try to see this as an opportunity to honestly assess yourself as a budding publishing professional. Remember that your boss doesn't expect you to find the next *YOU: The Owner's Manual* in the slush pile. Bosses know that entry-level people don't have much experience—that's why newbies start at the entry level. See the annual review as a time to learn what you do well and what you might need to work on. What kinds of things do you like or not like about your job? What are you good and not so good at? Are you ready for more responsibility, or are you totally swamped? Is publishing the right career for you?

Here are some tips on keeping your cool (and your perspective) during your review.

- **Repeat "nobody's perfect" to yourself.** It's true, and it means that your boss has to pick at least one weak area that you should work on. If your review came up 100 percent positive, the process would be totally meaningless. Your boss is there to teach you, so she'll definitely find at least one thing that you need to work on—otherwise she wouldn't be much of a teacher, huh? Remember too that you're a cog in a vast machine. Your boss has to help the department and the company function better, and she does this by giving everybody—even all-stars like you—critical feedback.

- **Don't focus on the negative, and don't take it personally.** So your boss thinks you make too many grammatical mistakes in your emails. That's not so bad. It's not like your supervisor told you that you're incompetent or a terrible person. She's only giving your work persona a little (helpful) tweak. Take a deep breath, buy yourself a grammar handbook, and keep it all in perspective.

- **Pay attention.** Before you leave the review, make sure you know what's expected of you and what behavioral changes your boss would like (or needs) to see. Say your boss tells you that you take too long at lunch. Accept the criticism, acquire a watch, and take less than an hour every day. Don't overreact and stop leaving your desk altogether.

- **Keep your eyes on your prize.** Don't worry about anyone else's review, even if you think so-and-so deserves a demotion. Similarly, while it's natural to feel jealous when a coworker gets promoted, don't get down on yourself. If you learn from your mistakes and develop a strong work ethic, someday you'll have your day in the proverbial sun.

- **Take deep breaths.** If you find yourself getting upset during your review, ask for a few minutes to collect your thoughts. Remember too that your boss will probably ask you to respond to the review in writing. That's your chance to share your side of the story, to accept the criticism with poise, and to indicate how you plan to improve. You'll probably also have a few minutes during the review to talk about all the things you did wonderfully over the year.

TURNING DOWN A PROMOTION

A promotion means all sorts of wonderful things: more responsibility, more money, a new title, a new work space. But a promotion might also mean that you'll be stuck doing more work you weren't really wild about in the first place. You don't have to accept a promotion simply because your boss offers one to you.

Here are some red flags that might indicate a promotion simply isn't the right step for you.

- **You have to relocate.** Maybe you have a girlfriend you'd like to be near, or you recently bought a co-op (lucky you). Maybe you want to be near your family, or maybe you hate the city you'd have to move to.

- **You'll have significantly different working conditions.** If you've been a sales assistant for a year and the company wants to put you out in the field, consider how much you like driving, eating out, and sleeping in hotel rooms. Could you do it 30 weeks out of the year?

- **The timing is lousy.** A promotion usually means more responsibility. Are you in a position where you can spend more time and energy at work? We're not talking about whether you'll have to bail on your Wednesday happy hours. If you have young children at home or are working toward an advanced degree, you may not be able to shoulder a load of new responsibilities.

- **You hate your job.** If you don't like the work you do as an editorial assistant, frankly, you probably won't like the work you'll be doing as an assistant editor. Carefully consider whether the promotion will lead you to a more fulfilling professional life.

If you do turn down a promotion or a lateral transfer, make sure the company knows how honored you were to be considered. Thoughtfully explain why you've chosen to stay in your current situation.

Be prepared

Your boss will probably give you several weeks' notice about your upcoming review. Use this time wisely. Go through old emails, and pull out any that praise you or something you did. (And if you're not saving those emails, start doing so *stat!*) Review old status reports, and write down concrete ways in which you impacted or affected the books.

Essentially, you need to collect data on your own performance. Make a list of projects you worked on, noting specific tasks you performed. Rather than say, "I worked on the backlist catalog," say, "I collated 80 titles for inclusion in the backlist catalog. Then I proofread the titles against the ISBN database and helped the marketing department draw up catalog copy for the entire test-prep line." Don't inflate your accomplishments, however. Be honest, but be explicit.

Finally, think about your own weak areas. Figuring out a few things on which you think you could improve will not only prepare you to hear your boss's criticism but will also give you an opportunity to show your boss how you plan to conquer those areas. For example, say you're not always up-to-date about the status of your projects. Tell your boss about how you recently ordered a dry-erase board, on which you'll list your projects using different colors for each stage. He'll be impressed with your initiative.

LEARN ON THE JOB

For some professions such as law or teaching, you need to sign up for years of additional education. Publishing's a bit different, however. Though some schools offer a master of science in publishing, most higher-ups in the industry don't have advanced degrees in the field. Many people enter the industry right after college, and then they learn on the job. But this doesn't mean that your education stops when you get your bachelor's degree. Au contraire: In many ways, it's only beginning. Treating your first job like graduate school lets you learn on the job—and relieves some of the pressure you might be feeling to do everything perfectly right away.

Seek a Mentor

Thrill seeker or not, you wouldn't want to go skydiving without an instructor, would you? And there's a reason why you have to take a test before you get a driver's license. Like skydiving and driving, working in publishing takes some time to understand. During your first year, you'll take some nasty spills and wrong turns, but your mentor will show you how to land and where to park.

A good mentor will make your publishing life much, much easier. She'll answer your questions, tell you stories about her background and professional development, and offer advice on everything from whether you should take a copyediting class to whether you should ask for a raise.

Some larger companies have formal mentor programs. Usually someone from your department, but maybe not your own team, will be there to answer your questions about everything from where to eat lunch on your own to how to replace your misplaced ID card to how to understand profit-and-loss statements during your first few weeks of work. If you're looking for a formal mentor in a large corporate setting, ask the human resources department about hooking you up with someone looking for a mentoree.

Less formally, you might also find yourself naturally gravitating toward a senior member of your department or company. Email to ask that person out for coffee or lunch. Be clear about your intentions, and say something like, "I really enjoyed your cover designs. Do you think we could get a latte sometime and talk about typefaces on jackets? I'd love to hear your thoughts on which fonts work best. My treat." If there's a meeting of the minds, and you get along well, you've just found yourself a mentor. Sometimes you have to take the first step.

Learn from Your Colleagues

While it's tempting to see your coworkers as nothing more than warm bodies whose food takes up valuable real estate in the office fridge, consider them instead to be repositories of information. They're vast resources of different experiences and knowledge, and they're most definitely a part of your network. Treat them as such by chatting them up at the coffee machine. Find out what they're working on, how their projects are going, and what kinds of things they like to do on the weekends. Ask them casual questions about where they worked before or what their first job in publishing entailed. Don't stalk them; be friendly and open. Eventually, you'll be able to move the conversations from, "I like that tie," to, "Do you have a few minutes to show me how to format the sales report in Excel? I really liked the sheet you handed out at the pub board last week."

Join a Professional Organization

Go ahead and be a joiner. Organizations such as Young to Publishing in New York City offer all kinds of opportunities for people new to the field, including happy hours with industry professionals. You'll get a chance to network with other first years while learning valuable information about the industry. Don't forget to get everybody's business cards. Some companies will pay for your membership if you can demonstrate the value of the organization to your day-to-day job.

You'll also want to hang out at industry events. Local schools often host panel discussions or have guest speakers present information on the job market. These talks and events give you the opportunity to ask questions, network, and make new friends—everything you need to stay up-to-date on industry trends. Make an effort to attend readings and literary festivals. If possible, attend BookExpo America, the largest gathering of authors and publishers. There you'll be able to rub elbows with famous writers, get free galleys of hot titles, and pick up catalogs.

Study Up

School never stops, at least not if you want to get ahead in your career. The best way to educate yourself about publishing is to read. Good thing you're working with books all day, eh? Seriously, though, reading helps you keep up your computer skills, master the *Chicago Manual of Style* and *Words into Type* (aka the two bibles of publishing), and understand everything there is to know about what your house's competitors publish. And you'll also want to read all the documents your house produces internally, such as catalogs and sales reports.

Read everything you can get your hands on. Check out what your company keeps in its library. Many companies have subscriptions to major publishing industry periodicals that you can read during your lunch break. Consider getting your own subscription to major trade publications such as *PW*. It's expensive, sure, but the opportunity to share a tidbit or two with your boss long before the rest of your coworkers have even seen the latest issue outweighs the initial cost.

Get educated by taking classes. Your company's human resources department probably sponsors lots of workshops. Sign up and learn everything there is to know about BookScan or InDesign. Similarly, your company might be willing to shell out for a night class or seminar so that you can learn a new skill and teach it to your coworkers. If you're in production, brush up on your copyediting and proofreading skills while on the company's dime. If you're a designer, sharpen your Photoshop techniques. If you're in publicity, take classes in event planning. Take the initiative, be creative, and educate yourself. You'll learn something, and you'll be able to add the class and the skill to your résumé.

THINK AHEAD

Gone are the days when you'd work for the same company for 30 years and retire with a nice gold watch and a fat pension. In fact, the average 20-something can expect to have as many as five different careers before she retires. The job market isn't what it used to be.

If you're serious about becoming the next Peter Olson, CEO of Random House, part of your game plan should involve mapping out your next step. Getting your first job is an awesome accomplishment, so spend some time acclimating yourself to your new work life. After a while, start thinking about job number two, even if you aren't necessarily ready to move. Assuming you don't report to your mentor, discuss next steps with your mentor. Generally speaking, you should avoid talking about next steps with your boss unless you hope to move up within the company. When it comes time to change companies or departments, you'll be glad you kept in touch with the people you work with, because as they move along in their careers, they'll be valuable sources of information—not to mention recommendations.

When to Move

Plan on staying at your first job for at least a year or two. Companies spend about 18 months getting a new employee up to speed, so you may not get a great recommendation from your boss if you suddenly announce that you're leaving after only six months. If you like what you're doing and you're learning from it, keep doing it, at least for a little while. You'll also want to show future employers that you've got staying power and "stick-to-it-tiveness," as our dad would say.

66 Do not stay in any job longer than three years without a promotion, no matter what they promise you. Some of the more tony houses are very reluctant to promote, and if you're not careful, you can find yourself staring down 30 as an editorial assistant. When you try to find another job, people will think you're overqualified, and it'll be tough, because you ARE overqualified. And you'll become bitter, which is also not helpful during a job search."

—An anonymous book scout

Eventually, you'll be ready to think seriously about leaving your job for a new position or new company. Make sure you answer the following questions honestly before you waltz into your boss's office with a letter of resignation.

- **Have I learned everything I can at this job, in this position, at this company?** Hint: The answer is usually "no." But if you've been at your job for around two years without a promotion and none seems forthcoming, it's probably time to move on. (For your own sense of self-worth, you might want to schedule a friendly chat with your boss to find out why you haven't been promoted before handing in your resignation letter.)

- **Have I participated in a whole year's worth of titles and lists?** If you haven't, potential employers might see you as flaky.

- **Is this a lateral move?** Upward moves—which are far more desirable—can be promotions within your current company, more prestigious positions at a similar house, or similar positions at a more prestigious house. If you're thinking of making a lateral move, consider the fact that you'll still have to spend time getting used to your new company's politics and procedures, so it can often mean

lateral move: A similarly titled job at another, similar company.

more of a setback than you might think. However, if you're currently working in children's books and you decide that your real calling lies in literary fiction, you may have to suck it up and take a similar job somewhere else.

- **What am I getting myself into?** See how well you can scope out the other job. Do the people there get along with one another? If you're replacing someone, why did he or she leave? Is it harder to get to the office? Here's where your network comes in. Ask people you know if they know anyone at this new company, then call up your new second-degree friends to (delicately) get the inside scoop.

- **Am I leaving for the right reasons?** Maybe your boyfriend is moving to Boston and you've decided to go with him. Maybe your grandmother is very sick and your family needs your help. Maybe you can't stand New York City. Those are all sensible reasons for leaving a particular job. If you're leaving because the hours are long or because someone got mad at or criticized you, you're running from a job, which is very different from running toward something.

- **Is it a personality issue?** Even though you yourself are an angel and a model of sensible professionalism, sometimes there are people at your job you can't stand to work with. If you've tried everything— being nice, asking for help on a project, offering to help on one of theirs—it might be time to at least talk with your supervisor about switching departments or teams. If the problem is with your boss, don't blab all over that you're not getting along, but do seek wise counsel outside of work.

- **How does this move fit into my long-term career objectives?** Every time you think about switching jobs, the step ahead should improve your life in at least one of these three areas: what you do all day, where you do it, or whom you do it with. If you're looking at a great opportunity that will open up even more opportunities down the line, go for it. If you don't have a clear sense of where the job might lead, carefully weigh the upsides and the downsides of both keeping and changing jobs. Bust out that pen and paper, and make a good old-fashioned list of pros and cons.

8

EXPLORING RELATED OPPORTUNITIES

T he road to success is paved with good intentions, of course, but it's also paved with lots of varied experiences. Trust us. Many an editor in chief got her start as a clerk at a bookstore, and not a few publishers began in the mailroom, as secretaries, or as sales assistants. Still others came up through the magazine ranks or began as book packagers. A freelance gig as a copy editor, designer, or writer sometimes leads to an in-house position. The world of book publishing encompasses much more than what happens inside a house. In this chapter, we explore jobs that let you gain experience and build networks. Heck, you might even find something here that you like better than a traditional job in publishing.

THE OTHER SIDE(S) OF BOOK PUBLISHING

Don't worry: We're not talking about anything illicit or shady. Rather, we're talking about key aspects of publishing that don't generally take place inside a publishing house. Yet without the folks who work in these positions, books simply couldn't get made.

Book Packaging

Book packagers, or book producers, are the publishing industry's best-kept secret. A packager usually handles every aspect of the bookmaking process, from hiring a writer to editing the manuscript to designing the interior and the cover to taking care of copyediting, line editing, and proofreading. The packager does everything relating to producing the book, then provides the publishing house with final packaged PDF files ready for the printer. Sometimes the packager comes up with the idea and approaches an agent or an editor with a polished proposal, and sometimes it's the other way around, with an agent or publishing house hiring a packager to execute a specific book or series.

Read any of these babies lately?

The books and series below were all packaged.

A-List
The Clique
Complete Idiot's Guides
Cooking Smart for a Healthy Heart
The Goosebumps series
Gossip Girl
The Hardy Boys series
Rolling Stones 40 × 20
The Sisterhood of the Traveling Pants
Sweet Valley High

And here's a list of some prime-time packagers.

Alloy Entertainment
becker&mayer!
Cader Books
Oomf, Inc.
Print Matters, Inc.
Welcome Enterprises, Inc.

To find out more, check out the American Book Producers Association's website (abpaonline.org).

Packagers often take on complicated book projects that publishing houses can't do in-house, such as intense graphic design books, packaged educational materials, or books that come with special products such as DVDs or packets of seeds (for a gardening book, say). But more and more, packagers function as one-stop shopping for books, movies, product tie-ins, CDs and videos, and television shows. As such, packagers have to be super-creative and incredibly market savvy. They need excellent project management skills, since they deal with every aspect of the production process, as well as superior people management skills, since they have to manage their freelancers and keep the publishers satisfied.

Freelance Editorial and Production Services

Some old-school publishing houses still have in-house copy editors, fact checkers, proofreaders, and indexers. But most companies today find it more cost-effective to contract that work out to freelancers instead of keeping people on staff. Production editors and other members of the production and manufacturing department manage these freelancers. Through their line editing, copyediting, proofreading, fact-checking, and indexing, freelancers often develop a close relationship with both the project and the publisher. Do good work and you'll get more of it. Do great work and you might land yourself a cushy staff job in editorial, production, or design.

The best way to get into freelance is to take a class in whatever it is that interests you. Classes in copyediting and proofreading will focus on grammar, punctuation, style, and usage, whereas classes in fact-checking will teach you how to verify everything about anything. Indexing is a unique beast, relying on special software and well-honed skills. An added benefit of a class is that your instructor will introduce you to people in the industry looking for freelancers. Definitely invest in the latest editions of the *Chicago Manual of Style* and *Words into Type,* as well as the most up-to-date version of *Merriam-Webster's Collegiate Dictionary.* Put them somewhere close, refer to them often, and revere these books as you would a bible, since that's what they are: the bibles of production editorial services. Once you've mastered the skills and familiarized yourself with the resources, offer your services to any company that puts things into print. Every written thing benefits from a copy editor and a proofreader, so there's no shortage of work out there.

LINE EDITORS

A line editor goes through a manuscript line by line, checking to ensure that it's effectively organized and complete, which is why line editing is sometimes called "manuscript editing." A line editor focuses on flow, sequencing, clarity, and concision. Line editors will do everything from checking that all entries in a bulleted list are consistently styled as gerunds, say, to reordering chapters and adding introductory text. Line editors often make significant changes to the manuscript, unlike copy editors and proofreaders, who usually have to run their changes by the supervising editor or production editor. Because so many editors at large commercial houses spend their days acquiring manuscripts, the actual editing frequently falls to line editors and sometimes even to copy editors.

❝ Freelancing is a bit harum-scarum—not getting a regular paycheck definitely is a downside of not having a regular office job—but I like the editing work (it's creative) and the copyediting work (it's fun to apply hundreds of rules and to subtly fine-tune a manuscript).

—**Karen Taschek,** Editor/Writer
Taschek Trade and Tech

COPY EDITORS

A copy editor checks a manuscript for consistency and correctness in style, grammar, and punctuation. He creates a **style sheet** for the manuscript, which lists the preferred punctuation, the spelling of words, and the style of proper nouns that the author uses frequently (Cold War vs. cold war, for example) and notes anything unique or unusual about the author's style of writing (maybe the author specifically requested that the word *résumé* always include accents, or the editor wants to see the series comma). A copy editor suggests textual changes to the author or editor for purposes of clarity. Most copy editors proudly identify themselves as anal and type A, because copyediting demands the application of little-known rules across hundreds of manuscript pages. This kind of work takes attention to detail, a keen understanding of the English language, and a love of finding mistakes. Copy editors also must be sensitive to both the writer's voice and the reader's need for clarity.

PROOFREADERS

In a recent article in *Salon*, Melissa Holbrook Pierson called proofreading "a school of haphazard erudition," because a good proofreader knows a little about a lot. A proofreader checks for errors once the manuscript has been typeset, or laid out in pages. A proofreader (also known as a "proofer") checks that the pages' text matches what was in the copyedited manuscript, rechecks for consistency and correctness in grammar and punctuation (using the copyeditor's style sheet as a guide), and makes sure that all major components—chapters, page numbers, illustrations, headings, and other parts of the book—are in the right place. Proofreaders also check that the design specifications were followed. Like copyediting, proofreading requires an excellent grasp of the English language and an eye for detail, but good proofreaders also get off on design. Proofers have to check such minutia as whether all chapter titles look the same or whether a drop cap crashes into the surrounding letters; they look at grammar, typography, style, and aesthetics. Proofreaders have to be able to work locally, on a word-by-word and sentence-by-sentence level, as well as globally, looking at the book as a whole. There's a lot of pressure on proofers too: If they miss something, chances are that the error will get printed in the final book.

❝ I love copyediting and proofreading. Some friends tell me it's because I enjoy picking out others' mistakes. I love that I can see a job or project in front of me come to a complete finish (at least from my responsibility)."

—Anne Heausler, Editor
Holt, Rinehart and Winston

FACT-CHECKERS

Fact-checkers have the very time-consuming but extremely important job of verifying that all supposedly factual statements (people, places, dates, events, and so on) are indeed correct. Did the Battle of the Bulge start on December 16 or 17? Both book publishers and magazine publishers employ fact-checkers. Obviously, no publisher wants to print erroneous information, but publishers also employ fact-checkers to prevent lawsuits. For example, if a tell-all memoir claims that socialite Muffy von Miffling II slept with her gardener, the publisher needs to double-check that info before printing the book. The job of checking facts in a manuscript or article requires speed, thoroughness, interest in a wide array of topics, lots of

In the bestselling novel *Bright Lights, Big City,* Jay McInerney narrates a fact-checker's descent into a depressing, drugged-out life.

general knowledge, resourcefulness, and the ability to do research properly. You'll also need to know your way around the Internet and be familiar with databases such as LexisNexis and JSTOR.

See page ???

Indexers compile the organized lists printed at the back of most nonfiction tomes and textbooks that help people locate information in a book. Indexes function like road maps, helping readers figure out where to find specific information. The process of creating an index can be very demanding. First, the indexer must read and understand each and every chapter of a book. Then she identifies and categorizes the stuff readers would be most likely to look up. Each concept, term, organization, and person gets its own listing, but the indexer must also think like a reader and list the information in logical ways. For example, an index to a political science textbook might include an entry for NAFTA that says something like, "See North American Free Trade Agreement." In other words, indexers have to include cross-references and alternate spellings just to make sure that readers find what they're looking for. By the way, it's often the proofreader's job to double-check that the page references in an index are correct.

Indexing requires a thoughtful, well-read individual who's hyper-organized. An indexer needs to constantly and consistently trace the same terms across many hundreds of pages, sometimes even thousands. There are professional training courses for indexers, but you don't necessarily have to take them to become an indexer. You must be skilled at using indexing software, however, so taking a class might ultimately be worthwhile.

Ghostwriting

Like book packagers, ghostwriters are another well-kept secret of the publishing industry. Ghostwriters write books, speeches, and articles for a client while the client gets all the credit. You know how sometimes you see a book written by a celebrity that also lists someone else's name on the cover? Well, it's a pretty safe bet that the nonfamous person whose name appears in smaller type on the cover or in the acknowledgments actually wrote the book. Most ghostwriters don't get their names on book jackets or any kind of credit. They sign a contract and, often but not always, a confidentiality agreement that stipulates the fee and requires them to keep their mouths shut about their participation in the project. Ghostwriting has been a common and acceptable practice in publishing for years; many people don't realize that a huge percentage of published books were written by someone other than the author. People hire ghostwriters because they don't have the time, skill, or discipline to write the book themselves, and they need someone else to turn write their ideas or stories into a structured and marketable book.

Ghost agenting?

Since early 2000, literary agent Madeline Morel has represented ghostwriters—and only ghostwriters. Editors call her with specific author needs, such as an expert in nutrition or a romance writer. Morel and her staff at 2M Communications, Ltd., then hook up the editor with a writer on her roster. She represents approximately 75 nonfiction writers, specializing in such fields as pop culture, parenting, and business. For obvious reasons, Morel doesn't name names, but her writers have been responsible for *The Biggest Loser* and *Jumping the Broom: An African-American Wedding Planner*, among other recent hits.

Becoming a ghostwriter takes time. You'll need to have a long line of publishing credits to your name before someone lets you write a book on his or her behalf. Start out small, by getting a few bylines in a local paper, then work your way up to publishing articles in the glossies. It helps too to have an area of specialization. If you can show a client that you're an expert in a field, that client might be more willing to hire you over someone with more experience. Craigslist frequently has posts from people looking for ghostwriters, so check out the listings there and on mediabistro.com.

❝❝ If what you really want to do is be a writer, do not become an editor. With a huge stack of reading on your desk every weekend, you aren't going to want to work on your own writing."

—**Julie Doughty,** Editor
Dutton

Book reviewing

Making money reading books? Who would have thunk it? It's true, and book reviewing is a great way to stay in the know about what's hot, hot, hot. You probably won't be able to make a living as a book reviewer, but you'll definitely gain some valuable knowledge about books. Editors and literary agents especially need to know how to quickly evaluate and summarize books, which is exactly what book reviewers do.

Book reviewing is a crucial part of the industry, since many consumers read book reviews to determine whether they will purchase a book. Publishing professionals read the trade reviews to see what the critics like and what their competitors are up to. To be a good book reviewer, you need to have excellent reading and writing abilities. As a reviewer, you have to both objectively describe a book and evaluate the book in some sort of context, be it cultural, historical, or literary. You have to do more than describe the plot—you need to take a stand, then explain how you arrived at that judgment.

To get started as a reviewer, offer to review a book that's coming out for your alumni magazine, college literary review, or a website you frequent and enjoy. Sweeten the deal by offering to do it for free. *Library Journal*, *PW*, and *Kirkus Reviews* rely on freelancers to get books read and reviewed. Reviewing books on BarnesandNoble.com or Amazon.com is another great way to build up your reviewing chops. Once you've gotten a few clips, send a query letter to the fiction or nonfiction editors at the aforementioned magazines to see whether they have a reviewing spot open.

"I've been reviewing literary fiction for *PW* for about two years. I love the opportunity to read stuff I might never come across otherwise, and I love giving rave reviews to books that deserve the praise. My editors give me two weeks to read a book and write a 260-word review that gives a good sense of the book's style, tone, and target audience. In return, I get to keep the galleys—and see my ideas (but not my name) printed in the magazine and at the online bookstores. I probably wind up only making about 10 cents per hour, but it's a fun way to earn a little extra money and stay in the know about what's coming out."

—**Jessica Allen**, Editor
SparkNotes

Technical Writing

For more information on technical writing, check out the Society for Technical Communication's website at stc.org.

Technical writers translate scientific and technical information into easily understandable language. They prepare operating and maintenance manuals, catalogs, parts lists, assembly instructions, online tutorials and help systems, and web-based training materials. These tech-savvy writers usually have a degree in or knowledge about a specialized field such as engineering, business, or any of the sciences. Many technical writers love all things technical but don't necessarily want to be an engineer, scientist, or programmer.

Although technical writers seem to lead a less glamorous writing life, they provide a necessary service and are usually rewarded handsomely for their efforts. Technically savvy people with the ability to express ideas clearly and logically for the average reader are a rarity—and the fast-paced world of technology ensures that there will always be jobs for people who know how to explain complex ideas to the average Joe Schmoe. For example, every time Apple releases a new iPod or operating system, they also need to release an accompanying manual, a set of tutorials, and training materials—and somebody needs to write all that stuff.

To obtain an entry-level job in technical writing, train yourself first by reading product documentation. Become familiar with the language; read "help" menus and manuals. Take classes in technical writing, web design, and programming. Proficiency in all Word features is a must; knowledge of Adobe FrameMaker and eHelp's RoboHELP is helpful. Be prepared for a lot of collaboration with the experts—engineers and programmers—under strict guidelines.

Business and Market Research Analysis

As a business, publishing needs to make money, so it longs to hire people who know how to make deals, spot trends, network and negotiate, develop new business models, and streamline operating procedures—all of which you can learn in business school, or "B school," as some call it. Business analysts examine all aspects of a company to increase efficiency and profitability. Publishers will hire an MBA to coordinate and oversee the opening of a new warehouse, for example, or to reconfigure the way books are handled at and sent to retailers from a distribution center.

Market research analysts try to determine a product or service's sales potential. They study past statistics, collate data on competitors, and conduct opinion research to determine public attitudes. Their research results help editors, publicists, and sales managers decide how to promote, distribute, design, and price products or services. If you're into statistics and data, market research might be perfect for you.

❝❝ As the market research analyst at Pearson Longman ELT, my task is to gather feedback from our customers (ESL teachers) worldwide and to synthesize it for our editorial team. I do this through online surveys/questionnaires, focus groups, interviews, and book pilots. About 40 percent of my time is spent on new projects or concepts, and 60 percent is spent on revisions and/or new editions. I also spend time researching trends (funding, enrollment, pedagogy, etc.)."

—Rebecca J. Ortman, Market Research Analyst
Pearson Longman English Language Training (ELT)

Human Resources and Recruiting

Human resources departments and recruiting agencies serve two clients: the employer and the employee. HR people interview, hire, and train employees for companies large and small. They often handle benefits and payroll, represent the company at career fairs, manage vacation policies, mediate between supervisors and employees in the event of a complaint, deal with sexual harassment issues, and make sure the company functions well from an administrative standpoint. The main purpose of HR is to ensure a good relationship between the employer and employee.

Recruiters match job hunters to jobs. Sometimes companies hire recruiters to fill positions, and sometimes job hunters hire recruiters to help them get hired.

Both HR and recruiting require excellent people and project management skills. You'll be dealing with people at all stages of their careers during a stressful time—when they're trying to find or just starting a new job. In addition to tact, you'll need sensitivity and enthusiasm. Public

Check out lynnepalmerinc.com to see a publishing recruiter at work. Since 1964, this company has placed job seekers at every level in the media industries.

For more information about human resources, check out the Society for Human Resource Management website at shrm.org.

relations, communications, human organization, and human resources are great majors for this field.

❝ I develop the company's diversity recruitment strategy, solidify relationships with relevant schools and community organizations, and augment our associations with our diversity partners such as INROADS, Prep for Prep, the New York Urban League, CityKids, and the Posse Foundation. I also chair our diversity committee, which is responsible for organizing employee events that raise awareness and foster an inclusive environment."

—**Francine Rosado-Cruz,** HR Diversity Manager
Penguin Group (USA)

Subsidiary Rights and Legal

The subsidiary rights department finds ways to make more money out of a book by figuring out other ways to use it—in other media, formats, or languages. Subsidiary rights include paperback editions, book club editions, foreign translations, magazine or newspaper excerpts, audiobooks, movie rights, e-books, and even computer software. The legal department helps negotiate subsidiary rights, as well as other stipulations in the author contract, such as royalties and advances. Legal also protects the publishing company from getting sued. The legal department reads manuscripts and copy to make sure they contain no libelous or legally objectionable material and makes any necessary changes to prevent a lawsuit.

Working in subsidiary rights or legal takes a type of savvy uncommon to most people attracted to the publishing industry. Think of it this way: If you weren't pursuing a career in publishing, you'd probably be pursuing a law degree or an MBA. Not only that, but you have excellent negotiating skills and also know how to mold a book idea into a sellable product in another medium. This position involves thinking outside the book pages.

Working in subsidiary rights and legal often serves as a great gateway into other departments. This isn't the most popular way of entering the field, so it's much easier to get jobs when you're just starting out. You may begin as a contracts or subsidiary rights assistant, both of which are primarily administrative but allow you to get a great deal of exposure to all departments. The experiences and skills that come from this exposure definitely come in useful in editorial and marketing/publicity. Remember: Combining a business mind-set with the ability to create and imagine will make you an unstoppable force in publishing.

ALTERNATE PUBLISHING CAREERS

Book publishing's not the only field that relies on writing and editing to get things done. Working for a magazine or a website is a great way to hone your communication or design skills. It's possible to springboard from a career in magazine or web publishing to a job in book publishing, but you'll have to show a book publisher you understand the difference between working with books, articles, and electronic content. Books often have a long production schedule—sometimes years—whereas magazines have a turnaround time of a couple of months and websites can be updated with new content in seconds.

Magazine Publishing

If you love the idea of writing, designing, or editing for a living but you're looking for a more fast-paced environment, check out the "glossies," as magazines are sometimes called. While both publishing industries use writers, designers, production people, and editors, magazines publish more frequently, are dependent on their advertisers, and require almost a crystal-ball-like understanding of trends (since magazines make money through their circulations, including subscribers and impulse buyers at newsstands and other outlets). Like book publishing, magazine publishing has long hours and so-so pay, but it also offers the satisfaction of producing a product that lots of people will read and enjoy.

FREELANCE WRITER
Some articles in magazines are written by in-house editors and contributing editors, but most are done by freelance writers. These writers must come up with a story idea, do some research, and then pitch the idea to an editor via what's known as a **query letter.** If she's interested, the editor

will hire the writer to write the story, giving the writer space parameters and working with the writer to fine-tune the idea or prose. The pitching process can be competitive, especially at the higher-end publications. And it can be tough to find just the right story idea that not only seems doable but will also appeal to a magazine's editors and readers. Sometimes an editor will contact an established writer to find, research, and write the story, although just about all published stories began as freelance pitches.

To get started writing for magazines, you'll need to collect **clips,** or samples of published articles you've written. If you haven't already written for your school paper or magazine, start by writing query letters to a local paper or magazine. Shortly but sweetly explain why your idea's worth pursuing—and why you're the ideal candidate to pursue it. The query letter acts as an advertisement for both you and the idea. An internship with a magazine will also let you get clips, as well as give you valuable contacts and knowledge about the field. If you're not into talking to people, you probably won't be into journalism. Freelancers also need to be comfortable with rejection: No one likes to hear the word *no,* but rejection is a fact of freelancing life.

66 Freelance writing is the ideal job for writers with widely varying interests and an appetite for deadline work in pajamas. I love working at home, because I find it much more efficient than going into the office—I gain two hours a day by skipping the commute and outfits alone—and I get to hang out with my pooch all day. I can also work for a wide variety of men's, women's, and general-interest publications at the same time, which is great for my peripatetic interests. You already know the work schedule—it's like college."

—**Arianne Cohen,** Freelancer for the *New York Times, Nerve.com,* and *Marie Claire,* among others

Web Publishing

The difference between writing and editing for the web and writing and editing books goes beyond just paper versus screen. Web content is shorter, caters to search engines, and must take into account the site's navigability. Editing and writing for the web requires the same talent for grammar, spelling, and style as editing and writing books, but web people need to understand how the site's visitors will move from one area to another as well. The information has to be presented in a way that will not only get visitors to the site but also keep those visitors hanging around. Websites make money by selling advertising, and advertisers don't want to buy space on sites with no visitors.

Everybody who works on the web needs to have expert knowledge of programming languages such as XTML or Dreamweaver. Web publishers also need an understanding of applications and content management systems, and they need to be able to see the big picture and figure out how to get other sites to link to their site. Aside from taking a class in web design or programming, another good way to get experience on the web is to create and maintain your own website.

Click, click, book

Many publishers have begun setting up their own retail websites, using Amazon.com, Powells.com, and BarnesandNoble.com as business models. These "D2C" (direct-to-consumer) sites specialize in books, but some sites, such Penguin's, also sell other stuff like tote bags and gift baskets. Houses that now make *and* sell books include biggies such as Random House and Simon & Schuster and smaller companies such as Tokyopop. This aspect of the rapidly changing nature of the publishing business guarantees that there will always be jobs for people with web backgrounds.

WEB DEVELOPER

Just about every company in the world has a website, and all those websites require web developers. Web developers create these sites, which involves coding the text into HTML (either manually or using a software program), programming, and often designing the site so that it is well organized, easy to navigate, and visually pleasing. That said, web developing tends to be more focused on the back end, on working behind the scenes to ensure that everything runs smoothly. Most web developers also have to continually update and maintain the site, since most sites contain information that changes on a regular basis. Web developers possess a unique combination of skills: network configuration, graphic design, marketing, project management, business, software development, and interface. Since web development requires such a wide range of responsibilities, several people usually work together as a web-developing team.

The best way to start out as a web developer would be to first learn programs that code or configure text for you, such as Visual Basic. Sharpen your graphic design skills by studying other websites. Take notes on why some sites work and why some sites suck. Every site you see had a developer, so learn from these people's successes and failures. Once you've honed your skills, make your own personal web site, then offer to design sites for friends and family. Build up a portfolio that includes sites for companies or individuals. If your portfolio shows originality, creativity, good navigability, and organization, you'll increase your chances of landing an entry-level position in web development. Web developers are needed everywhere, in every industry, so apply to any company whose products or services are of interest to you.

PART III: CAREER-PLANNING TOOLS

FURTHER RESOURCES

BOOKS

Book Business: Publishing Past, Present, and Future, by Jason Epstein, W. W. Norton, 2001
The inside scoop on the state of book publishing from an industry guru. Based on a series of lectures Epstein gave at the New York Public Library, this professional memoir-cum-industry-resource chronicles the industry from the nineteenth century on, and it offers Epstein's expert predictions on possible transformations in the future.

Bookmaking: Editing, Design, Production, Third Edition, by Marshall Lee, W. W. Norton, 2004
This tome tells you everything you'd ever want to know about editing, design, and production—or the three ways publishing prepares and transmits the author's words and meaning to readers.

The Book Publishing Industry, Second Edition, by Albert N. Greco, Lawrence Erlbaum Associates, 2005
A very objective, comprehensive, and thoroughly informative look at the state of the industry as it is today, filled with charts and tables. Everyone in publishing should own this book.

The Business of Books: How the International Conglomerates Took Over Publishing and Changed the Way We Read, by Andre Shriffen, Verso, 2000
A discouraging—yet provoking and realistic—look at publishing by the former head of Pantheon Books. Shriffen discusses what he considers to be the sad decline of American publishing while also offering a salute to the industry's original ideals.

Jeff Herman's Guide to Book Publishers, Editors & Literary Agents, Sixteenth Edition, by Jeff Herman, Three Dog Press, 2005
A book that's gone through 16 editions has got to be great, as this one definitely is. Like *Literary Market Place,* this book describes the various imprints, major media conglomerates, small houses, and agencies shaping publishing today. The information is perfect for aspiring authors and job seekers.

The Language Police: How Pressure Groups Restrict What Students Learn, by Diane Ravitch, Vintage, 2004
An eye-opening read about how the publishing industry affects education. Ravitch describes how right- and left-wing groups control the language and content of textbooks and standardized exams, often at the expense of truth, literary quality, and a comprehensive education.

On Publishing, by Lionel Leventhal, Greenhill Books, 2006
A professional memoir by the founder of Arms & Amour Press, the London Book Fair, and Greenhill Books. While recounting his lifelong journey through the publishing industry, Leventhal provides an inside look into British and intercontinental publishing.

A Short History of the Printed Word, Second Edition, by Warren Chappell and Robert Bringhurst, Hartley & Marks Publishers, 2000
A must-have for those involved in the design and production of books. Chappell's work investigates the history of typography, publication design, and printing techniques. The second edition's last chapter, written by Bringhurst, updates the book by discussing the digital revolution of the twentieth century.

The Truth About Publishing, by Sir Stanley Unwin, George Allen & Unwin, 1926
Timeless truths about the industry from the former president of the International Publishers Association. Most publishing professionals consider the principles discussed in this classic to be immutable, even as the industry changes so drastically.

ON-THE-JOB RESOURCES

The Chicago Manual of Style, University of Chicago Press, 2003
People in the know call this bad boy "CMS" or "Chicago." If you work in editorial, design, or production, this will be your bible. Updated roughly every decade, CMS covers all the details of the business,

from the publication process to distribution to marketing. Its rules of grammar and style have become the industry standard.

Literary Market Place, Information Today, updated annually
Ever wonder about the relationship among Fawcett, Ballantine, Random House, and Bertelsmann? Yeah, us too. This huge directory lists just about all the publishers in the United States and gives detailed info about imprints. Updated annually, *Literary Market Place* contains contact information for every major and most of the smaller publishers out there. Also check out literarymarketplace.com, which contains the world's largest, most comprehensive, searchable database of the publishing industry. By the way, Bertelsmann Book Group oversees Random House and Ballantine, which counts Fawcett among its imprints. Now you know.

Merriam-Webster's Collegiate Dictionary, Merriam-Webster, 2003
The dictionary used by all publishing professionals. For the most up-to-date version, log on to m-w.com to utilize the free searchable online dictionary. Better yet, register to have access to *Merriam-Webster's Collegiate* for a small monthly fee.

Words into Type, by Marjorie E. Skillin and Robert Malcolm Gay, Prentice Hall, 1974
A great companion to the *Chicago Manual of Style,* which is sometimes a

bit cumbersome, overwhelming, and tough to navigate. *Words into Type* covers manuscript protocol, copyediting, style, grammar, and usage, and it contains an easy-to-use index.

WEBSITES AND BLOGS

Arts & Letters Daily, aldaily.com
As the masthead boasts, this site features links to articles covering "philosophy, aesthetics, literature, language, ideas, criticism, culture, history, music, art, trends, breakthroughs, disputes, gossip." A great place to go if you don't know exactly what you're looking for but want to stay up-to-snuff on news and interesting stories around the world.

ArtsJournal, artsjournal.com
A daily digest with direct links to interesting stories from more than 200 publications featuring articles about arts and culture. Be sure to click on the "Publishing" link to narrow the choices. You can also have the digest sent to you as an email newsletter.

Authorlink, authorlink.com
A site whose objective is to be the "vital link between editors, agents, writers, and readers." It features a searchable database of news, resources, marketing services, author interviews, and book reviews.

Beatrice, beatrice.com
A blog written by a published author (and one-half of the GalleyCat blog). This book blog's primary goal is to introduce readers to writers. It features interviews with writers, short stories, author forums, author Q&As, and essays.

Booklist Online, booklistonline.com
Geared toward librarians, this site contains a searchable database of more than 100,000 book reviews. There's also a subscription newsletter available via email.

TheBookseller.com

Primarily a resource for publishers and industry professionals in the United Kingdom, this site has a ton of info about international publishing. It posts daily news and opinion, author interviews, career advice, recruitment opportunities, discussion forums, and bestseller lists. Also be sure to subscribe to its daily email newsletter, *TheBookseller.com Bulletin*.

Bookslut, bookslut.com

A monthly web magazine written by avid readers and writers. This blog is for those who love to read books, and it's become a go-to site for book critics and reviewers everywhere. It contains book reviews, columns, news, and author interviews.

The Book Standard, thebookstandard.com

The site of "all things book," including book-market analyses, sales figures, information about rights, and lists of deals. Publishers, agents, and authors frequent the site for its reviews, job boards, and news.

Booktalk, booktalk.com

An online book lovers' community that features personalized author homepages, as well as articles pertaining to writing and information on literary events. Each author page contains excerpts from bestselling novels, information about upcoming releases, author biographies, and agent and publisher information.

Book2Book, forums.booktrade.info/booktrade.php

A U.K.-based website founded by a group of publishers, booksellers, and journalists. It aims to provide news, features, and resources for professionals in the book-publishing industry, particularly in Britain.

BookWeb, bookweb.org

The website of the American Booksellers Association, an organization for independent booksellers. Be sure to check out Book Sense, ABA's program for promoting eclectic books chosen as noteworthy by independent booksellers; these books are known as "Book Sense Picks," discussed in a newsletter and printed on a widely distributed weekly bestseller list.

BookWire, bookwire.com
A great industry resource that contains extensive links and information on new books, authors, and industry trends. The site also posts book reviews, author video clips, and information about book events.

Critical Mass, bookcriticscircle.blogspot.com
Written by the National Book Critics Circle board of directors, this blog covers all things literary and critical. The posts are opinionated and sometimes controversial but always very, very smart.

GalleyCat, mediabistro.com/galleycat
A book publishing blog written by industry experts. It gives insider news, runs a comment section so that readers can discuss the posts, and has links to other helpful resources and blogs. GalleyCat is avidly read industry-wide.

Gawker, gawker.com
A great place for media, celebrity, and New York–based gossip. You can't beat the commentary from its sardonic writers, and this site will lead you to practically every gossip site in existence. If you're into that sort of thing, that is.

I Want Media, iwantmedia.com
A site featuring media news, resources, and industry data, continually updated throughout the day. Founded by a freelance writer and adjunct professor of journalism at NYU, this site tries to understand the implications of technology on media.

Mediabistro.com
A hot site for professionals in all media industries. Mediabistro.com is the creative professional's answer to monster.com. The site features job postings, industry resources, and forums as well as posts information about networking events, classes, and career development seminars.

Publishers Marketplace, publishersmarketplace.com
Be sure to sign up for their daily email newsletter, *Publishers Lunch,* for the

latest goings-on in the industry, including recent acquisitions. Consider too spending a few bucks a month for access to this comprehensive site. If you only read one newsletter, read this one.

Publishers Weekly, publishersweekly.com

The online companion to the must-read trade magazine. It's not as comprehensive as the magazine, but here you can subscribe to *PWDaily*, a daily email newsletter with updates on industry happenings and big deals.

Publishing Insider, publishinginsider.typepad.com

A blog written by an industry veteran who now works for HarperCollins. The content focuses not only on books but also on movies, music, art, and theater. It also tries to use and explore "word of mouth" as a way of promoting authors, musicians, artists, and actors.

Shelf Awareness, shelf-awareness.com

A blog and email newsletter designed to help people buy, sell, and lend books in stores, libraries, and online. The site is dedicated to letting buyers and sellers know what's hot, what deserves another look, and what's going on in the industry.

UnBeige, mediabistro.com/unbeige

An award-winning blog about all things related to design. It includes info on what's happening in book publishing, magazine publishing, and other media industries. There's a whole lot of links here too.

WritersDigest.com

This website is an online bible for writers seeking to publish their work. It features a bookstore, online workshops, information about writers' conferences, a book club, an email newsletter, and a link to the *Writer's Market,* a priceless database of editors, agents, and magazine masthead info.

TRADE PUBLICATIONS

Horn Book Magazine

A bimonthly magazine featuring book reviews and articles on children's and YA books. The same folks that run the magazine publish the book, called *Horn Book Guide,* semiannually; this book includes reviews of almost every children's and YA hardcover book published in the United States. Check out the website at hbook.com.

Kirkus Reviews

A biweekly publication containing reliable reviews written by specialists in relevant fields. It reviews 5,000 titles annually, including nonfiction, mystery, science fiction, and translations. Check out the website at kirkusreviews.com, and sign up for the free email newsletter.

Library Journal

The self-proclaimed "one-stop" source for library professionals as well as distributors in the library market includes articles and reviews of books, audiobooks, and DVDs. Check out the website at libraryjournal.com.

Publishers Weekly

If you read no other magazine on this list, read this one. This New York–based weekly covers the publishing industry in detail and publishes detailed bestseller lists. They also have a very comprehensive website at publishersweekly.com, which lists jobs, industry resources, book reviews, on-sale calendars, reviews, and the aforementioned bestseller lists.

Publishing Trends

A monthly subscription newsletter containing news and opinion on what's happening in the industry. The newsletter can also be emailed as a PDF. For more info, head to publishingtrends.com.

PROFESSIONAL ASSOCIATIONS

American Booksellers Association, bookweb.org

A not-for-profit organization for independent bookstores. ABA provides its members with education, advocacy, research/statistics, and general state-of-the-industry information; sponsors Book Sense, which compiles bestseller lists based on what's selling well at ABA member stores; and co-hosts an annual convention with BookExpo America each spring.

American Library Association, ala.org

The oldest and largest international library association. ALA seeks to promote high-quality library and information services and offers professional services and publications, including news stories and analyses of crucial issues.

Association of American Publishers, publishers.org

A trade association of book publishers, with a very extensive website of information about the industry. It also has a professional and scholarly division, as well as a group for those young to publishing, called Young to Publishing Group.

Association of American University Presses, aaupnet.org

A membership association of nonprofit scholarly publishers. Members receive access to professional development, industry research and analysis, cooperative marketing and promotion programs, a bimonthly bulletin, access to listservs, committee reports, and business and marketing handbooks.

Editorial Freelancers Association, the-efa.org

A national organization for freelancers in the publishing industry. Its members include self-employed editors, proofreaders, copy editors, writers, and researchers, among others. In addition to industry events and meetings, members benefit from an email discussion list, a newsletter, job listings, online courses, and benefits programs.

Partnership in Print Production, p3-ny.org

A joint operation between the Association of Publication Production Managers and Women in Production. P3 provides professional resources, educational opportunities, and networking events to professionals and students in the areas of print production, publishing, new media, and graphic communications.

PEN American Center, pen.org
PEN American is a chapter of the world's oldest human rights organization and the oldest international literary organization. The organization's main goals are "to advance literature, to defend free expression, and to foster international literary fellowship," and its members include translators, writers, and editors. PEN American also offers writing grants, promotes international literature, awards literary prizes, hosts forums, and sends famous authors to inner-city public schools.

PMA, The Independent Book Publishers Association, pma-online.org
A membership association of independent and smaller publishers and self-publishers, offering cooperative marketing opportunities to bookstores and libraries. PMA serves book, audio, and video publishers worldwide.

Small Publishers, Artists, and Writers Network, spawn.org
A membership association for publishing professionals, including authors, editors, publishers, illustrators, printers, and publicists. Members have access to a discussion group and a health plan, and they receive market updates and information about events.

Small Publishers Association of North America, spannet.org
A nonprofit membership trade association of small and independent press publishers and self-published authors. Members have access to educational opportunities and receive discounts on services designed to help increase sales, visibility, and profits.

Society of Children's Book Writers and Illustrators, scbwi.org
The largest international organization for people who write, illustrate, and publish children's books. SCBWI sponsors two annual international conferences, as well as regional events worldwide. Membership gets you entrance to these events, a bimonthly newsletter, awards and grants for works in progress, and access to print and online resources.

Women's National Book Association, wnba-books.org

A nonprofit professional association for editors, authors, booksellers, and book reviewers. WNBA's members include both women and men, and the group works to promote reading and support the role of women in the publishing community.

Young to Publishing Group, publishers.org/about/ypg.cfm

A subdivision of the Association of American Publishers, this organization caters to people with fewer than five years of experience in publishing. YPG creates a supportive community for entry-level people by sponsoring guest speakers, distributing an industry newsletter, hosting networking events, and sending out free galleys.

RECRUITERS AND JOB LISTINGS

Adecco Creative, adeccocreative.com

A subdivision of the international recruiter Adecco, this group was founded not too long ago as a creative services provider. It caters to many markets, including publishing, advertising, and public relations. A great source for designers and production specialists.

Bookjobs.com

Affiliated with the Association of American Publishers, this site lists job openings and internship opportunities, geared toward recent graduates. It also gives info about events around the United States.

CollegeGrad.com

A priceless resource exclusively for college students and recent college graduates. This award-winning site provides the most comprehensive entry-level job search content of any job site on the Internet.

Craigslist, newyork.craigslist.org, boston.craigslist.org, etc.

Looking for a job, apartment, and auto mechanic in the same city? Try Craigslist, the nation's bulletin board. Pick your city, then cruise to the job section.

Lynne Palmer Executive Recruitment, lynnepalmerinc.com
Since 1964, this agency has been placing qualified people into jobs
throughout the publishing and other media fields. Their clients include
large, big-name houses, as well as smaller independents, and they place
people in all departments, including editorial and human resources.

Mediabistro.com, mediabistro.com/joblistings
Probably the best site on the web for jobs in publishing and other media
fields. Mediabistro.com is the creative professional's answer to monster.com.
The site features job postings, industry resources, and forums, as well as
posts information about networking events, classes, and career development seminars.

Monster, monster.com
Get access to thousands of jobs around the country, including potentially
lucrative publishing gigs. You can even upload your résumé for free.

Publishers Lunch Job Board, publishersmarketplace.com/jobs
Along with mediabistro.com, this site is a must-surf for anybody looking for
a job in publishing. Run by the folks at Publishers Marketplace, this site
also provides info on major deals, recent hirings/firings/promotions, and
general industry news.

Ribolow Associates, ribolow.com
This recruiting agency specializes in the publishing and advertising
industries. Its sister company, Ribolow Staffing Services, also provides
temporary work for publishing professionals in transition, finding them
jobs in assistant editing, proofreading, copyediting, production, and
graphic design, among others.

The Write Jobs, writejobs.com
This site lists job openings in publishing, journalism, and other media
fields around the world. There's also a place for you to post your contact
information and skill set so that interested parties can contact you.

INDUSTRY GLOSSARY

AA: "author's alteration," or a change made to the typeset *proofs* by the author, as compared to an *EA* (change made by an editor) or *PE* (printer's error).

acquisition: The process in which an *editor* (usually an *acquisitions editor*) buys a book for a *publisher*; an acquisitions editor is said to acquire a *manuscript* for his or her house.

acquisitions editor: Primarily solicits and evaluates *manuscripts*. This *editor* often has a particular area of expertise, which he has honed over time, and he also has an extensive contact list of literary agents, writers, established authors, and other media professionals. Like the *publisher,* the acquisitions editor has a keen sense of growing markets and spends much of his time reading magazines, newspapers, and trade journals to keep track of trends and competing titles. Once the acquisitions editor acquires a book, he works with the author and sometimes the agent to fine-tune the manuscript for quality while also developing and supporting the marketing/publicity effort. See also *developmental editor* and *editor*.

advance: A payment made to an author by a publishing house as an advance against royalties.

advance reader copy (ARC): Bound, uncorrected *proofs*. *Publicists* send ARCs (also called "bound *galleys*") to book reviewers, book clubs, and distributors for *blurbs,* for reviews, and to generate buzz.

afterword: Final remarks on or about a book, usually placed in the *back matter* and written by the author or by someone else.

appendix: Additional supplementary material in the *back matter* of a book; often includes tables, charts, figures, or a *glossary*.

audiobook: A book in a recorded audio format, either on a compact disc or in the form of an MP3. Many printed books are available in this format and can be purchased online or at a bookstore. Audiobooks are usually more expensive than their printed counterparts but are popular among consumers who might not have time to read.

auction: The process in which a book is sold to the highest-bidding publishing house.

author (illustrator) biography: Information and accomplishments about a book's author or illustrator; usually found in the *back matter,* on the *back flap* of a hardcover jacket, or on the back cover of a paperback. Also known as the "about the author."

back cover: The area of a book that usually contains *blurbs,* a summary of the book's content, and a brief *author biography.*

back flap: The physical part of a *dust jacket* of a *hardcover* book; it usually contains a short *author biography,* author photo, or *blurbs.*

backlist: Books that were previously published more than one year ago but are still on the market for sale.

back matter: All printed material that appears in the back of the book after the main text. It can include an *afterword,* an *appendix,* a bibliography, a *colophon,* a *glossary,* an *author biography,* endnotes, and an *index.*

bibliography: A list of books or articles cited as resources by the author.

binding: The *back cover, spine,* and front cover of a book; literally, what holds a book together.

BLAD: "book layout and design"; a promotional item that the marketing/publicity team uses to generate buzz for a book. It usually includes a complete front cover and one or two sample chapters laid out and typeset according to the interior design.

bleeds: A way of ensuring that color extends all the way to the edge of a page; a printer will "bleed" the color by printing over the *crop lines.*

blues: A photocopy or print out of all the *pages* of the book printed from the final plates. This is the last representation of the book a *publisher* sees before the book is printed.

blurb: A favorable quote by someone like another author, an expert, or a book reviewer from a well-known publication about the book; usually printed on the front or back of book covers.

board book: A small, thickly paged book intended for infants and toddlers.

body copy: The major portion of text in a book, excluding *front* and *back matter*.

boilerplate: A publishing house's standard *contract* offered to an author and used as a starting point for negotiating final terms.

book signing: A public event, usually held at a bookstore, in which an author reads from his or her book and autographs copies for readers.

buyer: The person who decides which books and how many copies of each book to stock in a bookstore or *chain*.

catalog: A list of the titles a publishing house has published or will be publishing; as such, the catalog usually lists both *frontlist* and *backlist* books.

celebrity book: A novel or *nonfiction* work written by a well-known personality or well-established author. The guaranteed success of these (sometimes less literary but always very popular) titles give big publishing houses the wiggle room to take risks on books by no-name authors or esoteric subjects.

chain: A large company, such as Barnes & Noble, that owns many bookstores under the same name.

chapter book: A book using mainly text (and sometimes one line drawing per chapter) to tell a story, aimed at children ages 9 to 12.

chapter openers: Uniform methods of demarcating chapters within a book. They often use the same typeface and design elements throughout and sometimes include a quotation (known as an *epigraph*). The first word of the chapter's first line sometimes appears in a fancy typeface or in a much bigger font known as a *drop cap*.

college (higher-education) textbook: An *educational book* adopted by a professor or academic department, then purchased directly by the students at college, local, or online bookstores.

colophon: A list of production information, including details about typefaces used and artwork.

concept book: A picture book that teaches a basic concept—such as the alphabet or colors—to preschool-age children.

contract: A legal document detailing an author's agreement to sell to a *publisher* some or all rights to a creative work; it details the author's advance, compensation, and *royalties*.

copyediting: A line-by-line check of a *manuscript* to ensure accuracy in punctuation, correct spelling and grammar, consistent style, and proper organization.

copyright: The exclusive right to reproduce and distribute works of original expression.

copyright page: A page in the *front matter* of a book that contains information regarding *copyright,* permissions, the publishing house, and Library of Congress cataloging data.

crash: A term used to indicate a rushed production schedule. Sometimes publishers crash a book in order to capitalize on a trend or an event. Whereas a typical book might have a one- or two-year-long writing, editing, and production schedule, a crashed title might go from idea to bound book in a couple of months.

creative director: Establishes the overall artistic guidelines and quality-control standards for the *publisher,* maintaining these standards based on an understanding of the market and creative trends. He or she runs the design department and oversees all aspects of the design process from the original concept to the bound book. The creative director is responsible for understanding the editorial vision and communicating this vision to in-house and freelance designers. He or she assigns projects to *designers* and commissions freelance artists, illustrators, and photographers to create all the design elements for the book. Finally, the creative director also works with the marketing/publicity department to either create or oversee the creation of the marketing and publicity materials for the books published by the house. Also known as the "art director."

crop lines: The lines printed on a page or set of *proofs* that indicate where the pages will be cut by the printer.

dedication: A brief expression of gratitude to a person or group of people to whom the book is dedicated; generally in the *front matter* of a book and sometimes appearing on the *copyright page*.

designer: The person who designs all elements of the book, including the cover or *dust jacket,* page layouts, *title page, chapter openers, endpapers,* and *spine*—all according to a design theme that meets the requirements of editorial, marketing/publicity, and production. Depending on the size of the publishing house, different people design the cover and the interior of a particular book. The designer decides typefaces for the text on the inside as well as the *display type*. He works with production and manufacturing to determine which materials to use for printing and what special elements to include, such as cover embossing and interior colors. He commissions photographers and artists for cover and interior images and illustrations and cleans up and color-corrects photos and artwork with graphic design software.

developmental editor: Develops books and series, from concept to bound book. Often, the developmental editor commissions a book—that is, she thinks of an idea and then hires a writer to write the specific book she has in mind rather than acquiring a *manuscript* from an agent. Once the manuscript is in, she makes sure that it conforms to the original plan for the project, which might involve many back-and-forth discussions with the author about content and style. She also hires and manages freelance expert reviewers, who double-check that the content of the book meets industry standards. She plays an active role in the *line editing* and *marketing* of the book. See also *acquisitions editor* and *editor.*

direct mail: A method of promoting books by sending a brochure, flyer, postcard, or other printed material directly to a group of potential buyers.

director of production and manufacturing: Determines the specifications and production processes, establishing the overall production department plans and roles. He or she procures the raw materials for printing the books by maintaining relationships with suppliers and ensuring that they meet their obligations to the publishing house for quality, cost, and schedule. The director also manages most of the company's budget, as well as its technology assets, and negotiates some of the company's largest contracts, such as those with *typesetters,* printers, and *distributors.*

display type: The typeface used for the title, *chapter openers,* and other decorative text.

distributor: A company, such as Publishers Group West and National Book Network, that warehouses, catalogs, markets, and sells books to bookstores, libraries, and *wholesalers* on behalf of a number of small publishers; larger companies and the media conglomerates tend to have their own distributors.

division: A branch of a publishing company. A division is often referred to as an *imprint* of the company.

drop cap: The term used to refer to the first letter of the first word of a chapter when that letter appears in a much bigger font or much different style than the rest of the chapter.

dummy: A rough mock-up of a book showing how all *front matter,* text, art, and *back matter* will appear.

dust jacket: A plastic or paper cover that wraps around a *hardcover* book; *flap copy* and *blurbs* are usually printed on the dust jacket.

EA: "editor's alteration," or a change made to the typeset *proofs* by the editor, as compared to an *AA* (change made by an author) or *PE* (printer's error).

EAN bar code: The *ISBN* number in machine-readable form, encoded with product information and printed on the *back cover* or book jacket.

early reader: Up to 64-page, heavily illustrated books for children ages 8–11, meant to prepare them to read *chapter books*; early readers are sometimes also called "easy readers" or "beginning chapter books."

e-book: A book stored in a virtual library, then distributed and read in an electronic format. e-Books are usually purchased and downloaded online as a digital file and read on a computer or on a personal digital assistant (PDA). They're especially helpful for college students, who can store thousands of pages of reference materials rather than lugging around textbooks. This format is also slowly starting to replace the print format in the arena of professional and scholarly publishing.

editor: Works with production and monitors the process from manuscript to bound book. She has a hands-on role in shaping the manuscript into a marketable and readable product, working with the author on line editing, working with the designer on cover and interior design, and also writing *flap copy* and copy for sales and *marketing/publicity* materials. See also *acquisitions editor* and *developmental editor*.

editorial director: The person responsible for the overall editorial direction of a house or *imprint*. Ultimately, the decision about whether to publish a book rests with the *publisher,* but the editorial director (also known as the "editor in chief") has significant say. Basically, the editorial director runs the editorial department. She or he assigns responsibilities for implementing the editorial program, sets and approves its budgets, schedules and oversees its progress, and organizes the hierarchy, deciding who reports to whom and who handles which titles. She or he also is a liaison between the editorial and marketing/publicity departments, so the editorial director must not only have strong skills as an editor but also a thorough knowledge of market trends.

educational book: Anything that helps teachers teach and students learn falls into this category of book publishing. There are three types of educational books: *elementary and high school (el-hi) textbooks, college or higher-education textbooks,* and *study aids.*

elementary and high school (el-hi) textbook: An *educational book* purchased by school systems and given to the students for free to use during the academic year.

endpapers: Thick paper that binds the hard cover to the bound interior *pages.* They usually match the book design in color and sometimes have a special design relating to the book's concept.

epigraph: A quotation from another source, such as a poem or play, that appears on a *chapter opener.*

errata: A loose sheet detailing errors found in a printed book.

festschriften: Collections of writings by several authors as a tribute to a scholar.

fiction: Imaginative or creative writing.

flap copy: Text printed on the inside of a *hardcover's dust jacket.* This text may include a book summary, an *author biography,* and any *blurbs.*

forecasts: Predictions as to how many books will be sold.

foreword: An introduction to a book, written by the author or someone else, placed in the *front matter* of a book.

front flap: The physical part of a *dust jacket* that contains the *flap copy* of a *hardcover* book.

frontispiece: A decorative illustration appearing before the main text of a book.

frontlist: All the books published in the latest publishing season by one particular house or *imprint.*

front matter: All the text in a book that appears before the main text. It can include the *title page, copyright page, dedication, table of contents, foreword, preface,* acknowledgments, and introduction.

galleys: Page *proofs* of part or all of the manuscript that *editors* look over and send to critics, journalists, *publicists,* and bloggers in the hopes that they will choose to review or hype the book.

genre: A specific category of books, such as science fiction or self-help.

glossary: A list of terms and definitions relevant to the subject of a book; found in the book's *back matter.*

gutters: The space between the printed text and physical edge of the page.

hard copy: Paper copy of a book or *manuscript* (as opposed to a digital copy).

hardcover: Books that are sewn, glued, bound with cardboard covers, reinforced with stiff cloth, and covered with a paper *dust jacket.*

hi/lo book: Features less challenging text combined with a compelling story (known as "high interest"); this type of book attempts to coax hesitant readers between the ages of 8 and 15 into more active reading.

imprint: A smaller publishing house within a larger house or media conglomerate. Each imprint has its own personality, and its books usually focus on a select few *genres,* subjects, or formats. The imprint name functions like a brand, often indicating a certain level of quality associated with the titles and authors it publishes. Knopf, for example, is an imprint of Random House and publishes distinguished and classic fiction and nonfiction. Another Random House imprint, Fodor's, publishes travel guides.

independent bookseller: A retail shop, not owned by large companies and not part of a *chain,* that sells books to the general public.

index: An alphabetical listing of specific topics, people, events, places, and key words in a book and the pages on which they are mentioned.

in-store date: The date that a product arrives in the stores and is available on the shelves for purchase; also known as the "on-sale date."

ISBN (International Standard Book Number): An international, numbered identification system that provides a standard way for publishers to identify their products without risking duplication by other publishers.

juvenile books: "Coming-of-age" novels or *nonfiction* works focus on such topics as dating, fitting in, friendships, sex, drugs, self-esteem, school, and family relationships. Also known as *YA books,* they often serve as learning and coping tools for adolescents, usually between the ages of 12 and 18.

kerning: The space between letters on the printed page or set of *proofs*.

kill fee: A payment made to an author or illustrator when a publisher cancels a project.

layout: The overall design of a book's interior pages, including text arrangement, illustrations, graphics, title, page numbers, and font/typeface.

line editing: A line-by-line review of a *manuscript* by an *editor* or copy editor, which focuses on style, flow, sequencing, clarity, and consistency.

list: The books published in a particular sales season (fall, winter, spring, or summer). See also *frontlist* and *backlist*.

list price: The cover price of a book; also referred to as the "retail price."

literary agent: A book industry professional who represents authors and illustrators; the agent helps to develop and perfect the book *proposal,* then sells the work to a publisher.

literary fiction: Creative writing that's valued for its often intellectual or poetic prose, artistic quality, and craftsmanship.

managing editor: The liaison between production and editorial and who usually oversees a sub-department within the larger production and manufacturing department known as "managing editorial" or "production editorial." She acts as the central source of information for all other departments. Her other tasks include developing procedures for controlling the flow from *manuscript* to bound book; coordinating the progress of scheduling and production; overseeing the hiring of freelance copy editors, proofreaders, and indexers; and establishing editorial guidelines. The managing editor also assists in preparing the *publisher*'s budget and publication schedule, which contains all pertinent information for each book, including the publication month and *in-sale date*, author, title, *ISBN*, dimensions, and U.S. and Canadian prices.

manuscript (ms): The author's written material before typesetting.

marketing: At a publishing house, the department that deals with anything designed to reach a book's intended audience.

marketing campaign: A strategy for reaching a book's intended audience.

marketing/publicity director: Develops *marketing* and *publicity* objectives, policies, and strategies for each book and market. He has the very important and daunting responsibility of identifying the marketing/publicity capability of the *publisher*'s books, spotting trends, and integrating market research and information about product development. The marketing/publicity director gives his approval in every stage of the process, from book concept to design to the production process to the planning and implementation of promotion and publicity campaigns. He also *forecasts* and manages sales budgets and works directly with promotion and sales.

mass-market paperback: A smaller paperback book printed on low-grade paper and released in a high quantity at a lower price than a *trade paperback*.

middle reader: A book aimed at children ages 9–11.

monograph: A scholarly, short book of concentrated statements or summations of research findings.

movable book: A book for infants and toddlers that includes special built-in features like pop-ups, foldout pages, liftable flaps, and hidden sound chips; also known as a *novelty book*.

niche marketing: The process of marketing and promoting a book to a specific group of buyers, such as a particular age group, demographic, or type of enthusiast.

nonfiction: Factual writing; writing that's true.

novelty book: A book for infants and toddlers that includes special built-in features, such as pop-ups, foldout pages, liftable flaps, or hidden sound chips; also known as a *movable book*.

option clause: A clause in a *contract* giving the publisher the right to consider acquiring the author's next book before other publishers.

out of print (OP): Occurs when a publisher no longer has copies of a book and has no intention of reprinting it.

overrun: The excess quantity of books that occurs when a *print run* is larger than the one ordered.

pages: The complete typeset pages of a book that goes out for review before the book goes to press; also known as *proofs*.

P&L: An accounting statement that calculates costs for production of a book, including profit and loss. Editors prepare "profit-and-loss" reports for all of their projects to estimate price, costs, specs, discounts, and, most important, potential profit.

PDF: "portable document format"; a way of electronically saving *manuscript* pages or *proofs* so they may be viewed on-screen but not altered or changed.

PE: "printer's error"; a mistake made by the typesetter or printer, including corrections that were marked but were not actually made or other errors, such as smudges, smears, and ink blots on *pages*. See also *AA* (change made by an author) and *EA* (change made by an editor).

permissions: Agreements from *copyright* holders granting someone else the right to reproduce their work.

picture book: A heavily illustrated book with a few lines of text per page, aimed at preschool-age children.

platform: An author's ready-made, built-in audience. For example, Oprah's platform for her books and magazines is the people who watch her television show. *Marketing* and *publicity* departments often work with *editors* to develop an author's platform.

popular (pop) fiction: A type of creative writing that is lighter than *literary fiction* and often formulaic, written to fit the style of a given genre, or category; also known as commercial *fiction*.

preface: The introductory text of a book written by the author.

prepress: The process of preparing a book for printing, including scanning images, creating *proofs,* and conforming color specifications.

press check: The critical final stage of printing, when someone from the production team travels to the printer on-site in order to approve samples of the printed *pages* while they are on the press. Adjustments can often be made on the press to ensure that colors print as expected.

press kit: A folder containing promotional materials (excerpts, reviews, and *press releases*) about a forthcoming book, distributed to the news media and other targeted outlets.

press release: A written announcement meant to draw media attention to a specific event or product launch.

print run: The number of books to be printed.

production editor: Manages *manuscripts* through the production process. She copyedits—or hires a freelance copy editor—to check the manuscript for style, consistency, spelling, grammar, and punctuation. She maintains direct contact with the *editors* to resolve any issues involving inconsistencies in style and information. Once the manuscript is typeset, the production editor proofreads—or hires a freelance proofreader—to check the page *proofs* for errors. In addition to monitoring the production process of the books' interiors, the production editor proofreads the covers, jackets, and *marketing/publicity* materials for the books. The production editor must also keep track of the progress of all titles and prepare status reports for the *managing editor*.

production supervisor: Manages the creation of the actual book. He develops and manages production schedules and budgets. He also secures estimates based on project specifications and selects vendors based on these estimates and consults with *editors* on specifications for paper, cloth, binding, and typography. The production supervisor, along with the *managing editor, traffics* materials through and monitors all stages of production to ensure quality, accuracy, and timeliness of the final bound book.

professional book: A book that serves as an educational tools in a specific profession or trade.

promotion manager: Schedules advertising, *direct mail*, exhibits, and promotional activities. She also maintains contact with all media outlets, reviews industry reports, and consults on *catalogs*, in-store displays, and all sales and *marketing/publicity* tools. The promotion manager works directly with the *editorial director* and *marketing/publicity director* to coordinate promotional, publicity, and marketing activities.

proofreading: Checking for errors once the *manuscript* has been *typeset*, with a focus on typographical issues in addition to other grammatical and stylistic errors that might have been missed during *copyediting*.

proofs: The complete typeset book that goes out for review before the book goes to press; also known as *pages*.

proposal: A description of a book that an author sends to an agent or publisher. It explains what the book is about, why people will buy the book, and why the author should be the person to write the book. It usually includes sample chapters and a *table of contents*.

pub board: Short for "publishing board," the group at a publishing house composed of representatives from sales, marketing, editorial, and finance, which approves the *acquisition* of a book.

pub date: Short for "publication date," or the date that a book will be available to consumers, typically a few days after the book's arrival in stores.

public domain: Intellectual property (books, inventions, computer programs, songs, movies) that is not legally protected, so that anyone may reproduce, sell, or otherwise use it without having to first obtain permission.

publicist: The person in charge of each book's *publicity* campaign. Publicists generate a buzz about the book even before it's published to ensure that there will be strong reader interest once the book hits the shelves. They also send *advance reader copies* to book reviewers at newspapers and magazines, radio stations, television talk shows, and websites. Finally, publicists create *press kits,* which contain pertinent information about the book, the author, and any selling points that would encourage members of the press to give the book exposure.

publicity: At a publishing house, the department that deals with anything designed to generate buzz about a book in the culture at large.

publicity campaign: A series of events held to create a buzz about an author or a book.

publisher: The head of a publishing house or, in a big house, of an *imprint*. The publisher ultimately decides which books get published. She or he also controls the purse strings and has final say on all budgets and finances. The publisher has a strong editorial, financial, and *marketing/publicity* background, and she or he is responsible for the overall direction—and profits!—of the house or *imprint*.

recto: The right-hand page of a book.

returns: Unsold copies of a book that are returned to publishers from booksellers.

revisions: Changes to a *manuscript* or other written work.

royalties: A percentage of a book's sales paid to the author or illustrator.

running feet: The text at the bottom of every page that lists the page number, name of the author or book, or title of the chapter or section.

running heads: The text at the top of every page that lists name of the author or book, or title of the chapter or section.

sales call: A meeting between the publisher's *sales representatives* and a potential *buyer*, in which the rep presents the sales *catalog* and encourages the buyer to purchase books.

sales channels: The best places for a book to be sold.

sales director: Oversees the entire sales force. She recruits, trains, and motivates the *sales representatives*; conducts sales meetings; and assigns territories. She develops budgets and *forecasts*, introduces the new books to the *sales reps*, and compiles field reports for analysis. The sales director, along with the *marketing, promotion,* and *publicity* managers, also influences the creation of book jackets and promotional materials, and she works with *marketing/publicity* in the creation of the sales *catalog*. Finally, she maintains consistent contact with major bookstore *chains, distributors,* and other important *sales channels.*

sales representative: Visits bookstores, libraries, schools, colleges, and other *sales channels* to encourage and take orders from seasonal sales *catalogs*. In order to become well versed in the house's or *imprint*'s titles, the sales rep attends seasonal sales meetings, where he or she gets the sales materials, including the sales *catalog*, order forms, promotional materials, and sales kits, which include a mock-up of every book cover and details about each book. The sales rep then travels to customers, pitching to book *buyers* and at trade shows and conferences. Larger publishers have their own house reps, who are salaried and whose expenses are paid, while smaller publishers hire independent reps on commission. The sales rep also has the very important responsibility of representing the publishing company to the wholesale-buying market. He or she becomes the face of the publisher, as well as its eyes and ears, regularly reporting back from the "field" on sales data and retail trends. In turn, analysis of those trends often drives the editorial development process.

slugging: A line-by-line comparison of the typeset *proofs* against the *manuscript* to make sure that no text was dropped and to ensure that the type was set according to the specifications.

slush pile: Unsolicited *manuscript* submissions received by publishing houses; usually editorial assistants are assigned the task of reading through and responding to the submissions.

special sales: Nontraditional sales in outlets, such as hardware stores, clothing stores, and pet stores, that do not specialize in book retail.

spine: The part of the book that faces out when it's shelved.

spread: A *verso* and a *recto*; two pages that face each other.

STM publishers: "Science, technical, and medical publishers"; publish professional books.

study aids: Materials used by students to bone up for a particular course or to prepare for a standardized test such as the SAT or the GRE.

submissions: *Manuscripts* sent by an author or *literary agent* to a publisher for consideration.

subsidiary rights: Rights to distribute a book in a different form, such as packaged for book clubs, as foreign translations, through excerpts in newspapers and magazines, or as a movie adaptation.

table of contents: A list in the *front matter* of the topics covered in the book as arranged by chapter and/or section, including the corresponding page numbers.

target audience: The specific group of readers likely to be interested in a particular book.

template: A standard design for use in line extensions.

title: A synonym for "book."

title page: Odd-numbered, right-hand page that lists the book's title, subtitle, author's name, and publisher.

trade books: Books aimed at the general consumer, rather than at a more specialized market, such as scholars or professionals. Sold to libraries, bookstores, and wholesalers or retailers (such as Costco, Wal-Mart, and Kmart), trade books can be either *fiction* or *nonfiction*, adult or children's.

trade paperback: Glue-bound books with a heavy paper cover; they tend to be larger, of higher quality, and more expensive than *mass-market paperbacks* but cheaper than *hardcover* books.

traffic: The act of monitoring materials as they move from one stage to the next during production. Sometimes this involves literally bringing a *manuscript* or set of *proofs* from one department to another.

transmit: The act of turning a *manuscript* over from one department to another as it moves through the production process. An *editor* transmits the manuscript to a *production editor,* for example.

trim size: The outer dimensions, usually in inches, of a finished book. The trim size of *Spark Your Career in Book Publishing* is 7.5 × 9.125.

typesetter: The person who lays out the pages as they will appear in the finished book.

typesetting: Occurs when a *manuscript* has been laid out into *pages,* according to the specifications of the *layout* and final design. The *typesetter* does the typesetting.

underrun: A finished order containing fewer books than requested.

verso: The left-hand page of a book.

wholesaler: A company, such as Baker & Taylor or Ingram Book Group, that buys books in large quantities from publishers at high discounts and sells them to bookstores and libraries at a mid-level discount.

YA books: "Coming-of-age" novels or *nonfiction* works that focus on such topics as dating, fitting in, friendships, sex, drugs, self-esteem, school, and family relationships. Also known as *juvenile books,* they often serve as learning and coping tools for adolescents, usually between the ages of 12 and 18.

CAREER-PLANNING WORKBOOK

MY CONTACTS

Keep notes about all the people you add to your network—if you're meeting as many people as you should, you won't be able to remember all their details! When you reconnect with someone a few days, weeks, or months after your initial meeting, a brief reminder of where and how you met will make it more likely that you'll get a response. Keep track of the email correspondence you have with these contacts: Start a folder in your email program titled *Job Search,* and stash all your messages there in case you need to refer to them later.

Name: Stephanie Carrelli

Company: Vintage

Title/Department: Assistant editor

Where We Met: Jonathan Franzen reading at the Strand

Follow-ups: emailed 8/23 to recommend *The Discomfort Zone*

Notes: likes memoir; might be opening in editorial this fall!

~~~~~~

Name:

Company:

Title/Department:

Where We Met:

Follow-ups:

Notes:

Name: _____

Company: _____

Title/Department: _____

Where We Met: _____

_____

Follow-ups: _____

_____

Notes: _____

_____

~~~~~~

Name: _____

Company: _____

Title/Department: _____

Where We Met: _____

_____

Follow-ups: _____

_____

Notes: _____

_____

Name:

Company:

Title/Department:

Where We Met:

Follow-ups:

Notes:

~~~~~~

Name:

Company:

Title/Department:

Where We Met:

Follow-ups:

Notes:

Name: _____

Company: _____

Title/Department: _____

Where We Met: _____

_____

Follow-ups: _____

_____

Notes: _____

_____

~~~~~~

Name: _____

Company: _____

Title/Department: _____

Where We Met: _____

_____

Follow-ups: _____

_____

Notes: _____

_____

COMPANY RESEARCH

BONUS TIP: Start a folder on your computer where you store electronic copies of any articles or press releases about the company.

Got an interview coming up? Knock their socks off by showing just how much you know about the company and its projects. After you impress them with your expertise, how could they help but hire you? You can also use these pages to collect research on any companies you'd like to be interviewing at someday.

Company: Farrar, Straus and Giroux

Contact: Cliff Smith, sales rep. csmith@ffssgg.com

History: Trade house since 1946. Really respected. Big on poetry, lit. fiction, and some nonfiction. 21 Nobel Prize winners in lit!

Major Competitors: Knopf, Vintage, Pantheon, HarperCollins

Significant Projects: *Dirty Blonde* (Courtney Love's journals), *The Echo Maker* (Richard Powers, 9/11 fiction)

Recent News: *Red Light Winter* (play) finalist for 2006 Pulitzer Prize

Other Notes: Imprints: North Point Press, Hill and Wang & Faber and Faber

Company:

Contact:

History:

Major Competitors:

Significant Projects:

Recent News:

Other Notes:

Company: _____

Contact: _____

History: _____

_____

Major Competitors: _____

Significant Projects: _____

Recent News: _____

_____

Other Notes: _____

_____

~~~~~~

Company: _____

Contact: _____

History: _____

_____

Major Competitors: _____

Significant Projects: _____

Recent News: _____

_____

Other Notes: _____

_____

Company: _____

Contact: _____

History: _____

_____

Major Competitors: _____

Significant Projects: _____

Recent News: _____

_____

Other Notes: _____

_____

~~~~~~

Company: _____

Contact: _____

History: _____

_____

Major Competitors: _____

Significant Projects: _____

Recent News: _____

_____

Other Notes: _____

_____

Company: _____

Contact: _____

History: _____

_____

Major Competitors: _____

Significant Projects: _____

Recent News: _____

_____

Other Notes: _____

_____

~~~~~~

Company: _____

Contact: _____

History: _____

_____

Major Competitors: _____

Significant Projects: _____

Recent News: _____

_____

Other Notes: _____

_____

RÉSUMÉ WARM-UP

List the classes, jobs, and experiences you've had that demonstrate your proficiency in the following areas. (For more specific guidelines, see Chapter 3.) Remember, your experiences don't all have to be industry related! During your three years as a customer service rep at the Apple store, you learned valuable people and communication skills that can transfer to any job.

On the following pages, write down whatever you can think of, even if you're not entirely sure it's applicable. You can always choose to focus on certain jobs and experiences when you actually write your résumé.

Creative Skills

_____

_____

_____

_____

_____

_____

_____

_____

Computer/Technical Skills

_____

_____

_____

_____

_____

_____

_____

_____

_____

_____

_____

_____

_____

_____

_____

Business Skills

People Skills

_____

_____

_____

_____

_____

_____

_____

_____

_____

_____

_____

_____

_____

Organizational/Office Skills

RÉSUMÉ ACTION WORDS

Your résumé is a marketing tool, so strive to make it a compelling advertisement for yourself. After you've written down all your relevant experience, use the list of keywords below to make your work sound as active and impressive as possible (without lying, of course!).

Also make sure to break down your job into specific duties. Rather than just listing "Camp Counselor" on your résumé and calling it a day, take a few extra minutes to articulate everything you were responsible for: *Supervised thirty 10–12-year-olds; coordinated daily swim sessions and sports events; developed three-month leadership program for older students; wrote weekly newsletter for parents.*

accelerated	designed	led	reorganized
activated	devised	maintained	reported
adapted	directed	managed	represented
administered	documented	mastered	researched
analyzed	drafted	maximized	responsible
applied	edited	modeled	reviewed
approved	eliminated	modified	revised
arranged	established	motivated	scheduled
assembled	evaluated	negotiated	set up
assisted	examined	organized	shaped
built	executed	operated	simplified
compiled	expanded	overhauled	solicited
completed	facilitated	oversaw	solved
composed	formulated	participated	streamlined
conceived	founded	performed	structured
conceptualized	generated	planned	supervised
conducted	guided	prepared	supported
consolidated	handled	presented	surveyed
constructed	illustrated	produced	synthesized
consulted	implemented	programmed	taught
contributed	improved	promoted	trained
controlled	increased	proposed	tested
coordinated	initiated	proved	translated
created	interacted	publicized	utilized
critiqued	interpreted	published	volunteered
delegated	introduced	recommended	worked
developed	launched	reduced	wrote

INTERVIEW WARM-UP

During your interviews, it's pretty much guaranteed that the following questions will pop up—a lot. So prepare your answers now, before you're in the hot seat.

Tell me about yourself.

_____

_____

_____

_____

_____

_____

_____

Why do you want to go into the publishing industry?

_____

_____

_____

_____

_____

_____

What do you know about our company?

_____

_____

_____

_____

_____

_____

Make sure you tailor your answers to the specific company you're interviewing for!

Why do you want to work at this company?

_____

_____

_____

_____

_____

What are some of your favorite writers or books? Why?

_____

_____

_____

_____

_____

_____

What are your strengths?

_____

_____

_____

_____

What are your weaknesses?

_____

_____

_____

_____

When and how do you do your best work?

_____

_____

_____

_____

_____

Tell me about a time when you had to overcome a difficult situation.

_____

_____

_____

_____

_____

What inspires you?

_____

_____

_____

_____

Tell me about your internships.

_____

_____

_____

_____

Where do you see yourself in five years?

_____

_____

_____

_____

_____

_____

_____

_____

Do you have any questions for me?

_____

_____

_____

_____

_____

_____

_____

_____

Your 5 Talking Points

Interviews often go by in a big blur, and 30 minutes later you're standing in the lobby thinking, *What just happened?* Learn from the politicians: Before you walk into an interview, think of the five things you most want to emphasize. Maybe it's the fact that you handled a full courseload while juggling two part-time jobs. Maybe it's the fact that you wrote your senior essay on John Edgar Wideman. Maybe it's the great transferable skills you gained volunteering at the animal shelter. Whatever they are, note them here. But don't go crazy and list everything impressive about yourself! Force yourself to focus on the most important things.

1. _____

2. _____

3. _____

4. _____

5. _____

Your 30-Second Biography

Sometimes, you don't get much time to make a big impression. Can you paint a vivid, compelling portrait of yourself in less than a minute? Write your 30-second biography in the space below. Memorize it. Use it.

_____

_____

_____

_____

INTERNSHIP TRACKING SHEET

Date	Company	Department	Contact Name	Contact Info	Reference Name	Activity	Next Step

JOB SEARCH TRACKING SHEET

Date	Company	Department	Contact Name	Contact Info	Reference Name	Activity	Next Step